God's Love Language
THE BIBLE'S INSTRUCTIONS ON HOW TO SPEAK IT

April Ray

GOD'S LOVE LANGUAGE

Snowbound ©2019 April Ray
Cover Design by Virginia McKevitt, www.virginiamckevitt.com
Formatting by Cordially Chris Author Services

TABLE OF CONTENTS

Prayer For The Reader 1

Brass Tacks 3

But The Laws Were Abolished 15

We are Gentiles...right? 31

But What About The New Covenant? 41

But the Law Was Made Too Hard 49

But Paul Said… 53

Repentance is a U-turn 69

Dems Da Rules 79

Food Fight! 113

The Mo-ha what now? 129

Are the Holidays Holy? 169

The Narrow Path … a Warning 203

Great resources for help in understanding Torah: 212

Recipes 213

    Mel's Fried Matzo 214

    Nikki's Matzo Toffee 215

    Nikki's Smoked Passover Lamb 216

    Easy Challah Bread 217

    Roast leg of Lamb au Jus 219

    Braised Brisket 221

    Ropa Vieja 223

Hummus 225

Unleavened Bread (Sweet version) 226

Acknowledgements 227

About April Ray 231

PRAYER FOR THE READER

Dear Heavenly Father,

I pray that Your influence and inspiration is found throughout this book, that nothing written will do anything but bring glory to You and Your kingdom. Abba, please remove any scales or preconceived notions that the reader may have when opening this book. Remove the scales from their eyes and do not let their hearts wax cold. Let this book be a blessing in their lives. Please protect them as they try to understand Your word and have a stronger relationship with You. Let them be as a Berean and research Your words for themselves and find the truth. Let them have a heart of flesh and not of stone. Let them hear the truth in Your word, have discernment and understand it.

In Yeshua's name, Amen.

BRASS TACKS

***Matthew 22:35-38** And one of them, a lawyer, asked him a question to test him. "Teacher, which is the great commandment in the Law?" And he said to him, "You shall love the Lord your God with all your heart and with all your soul and with all your mind. This is the great and first commandment."*

About five years ago, before my husband and I were married, he challenged me to read a book about love languages. It is a great book, and gives the reader a chance to look at themselves and how they perceive and understand love. My only disagreement with it was this— people change. At least most people do. People grow, mature and understand more as they progress through life. My love language at eighteen was vastly different than my love language was at twenty-eight. Hopefully, if I have learned more and become better, it will be vastly different at thirty-eight. It's been my experience that the human condition is selfishly based; meaning that even when they love someone, it is because of what they do or could do for you. Even if that isn't the truth ten years into a marriage, it probably started out that way. Your spouse made you feel good. They made you feel smart or sexy or special in a way that no one else could or would. YHWH willing, at year ten they still make you feel that way and always will, but it has grown into what can I do for them to make them feel the same way or better than I do with them. How can I show my appreciation for the feelings they give me?

We as humans are always changing. So, we have to adapt and relearn how to love our spouse, children, family, and friends because everyone changes and grows. For this reason, we tend to view God through those same glasses.

We believe how He feels love changes, because we as a society have changed. We now have Him accepting practices and conditions that a thousand years ago He wouldn't have accepted, because OUR views have changed. But what does the Bible say about that?

Numbers 23:19 *God is not human, that he should lie, not a human being, that he should change his mind? Does he speak and then not act? Does he promise and not fulfill?*

Hebrews 13:8 *Jesus Christ is the same yesterday and today and forever.*

James 1:17 *Every good gift and every perfect gift is from above, coming down from the Father of lights, with whom there is no variation or shadow due to change.*

Malachi 3:6-7 *For I am the LORD, I change not; therefore ye sons of Jacob are not consumed.*

Even from the days of your fathers ye are gone away from mine ordinances, and have not kept them. Return unto me, and I will return unto you, saith the LORD of hosts. But ye said, Wherein shall we return?

So, what can we determine from these verses? YHWH (LORD in your Bibles always stands for YHWH/YHVH) does not change. He doesn't need to; He is Alpha and Omega. He has seen what is coming and saw it before the Earth was formed. He is not like us in that way. He doesn't have to learn, grow or become better than how He started. He doesn't need to learn how to love us because He already knows how. We need to learn to love Him. Luckily for us, He is unchanging, and He gave us the love instructions in the Bible.

At the start of this chapter, I added Matthew 22:35-38, what Yeshua (Jesus) Himself said was the greatest of the commandments, to love YHWH. It doesn't say that the greatest is His love of us or the grace of his love, but to Love HIM. So how do we love him? Over the next few pages, we will discover the Bible verses that tell us exactly how to do so.

John 14:15 If you love me, you will keep my commandments.

Well, that seems pretty straight forward doesn't it? Close the book.

You are probably saying to yourself, "Well I got ripped off just to learn I need to follow the ten commandments! I do that already!"

If it were that easy, I wouldn't be writing this

book. So, let's continue, shall we? There are eight different scripture passages that specifically tell you the same thing. The two already stated and the following:

John 14:21 *"Whoever has my commandments and keeps them, he it is who loves me. And he who loves me will be loved by my Father, and I will love him and manifest myself to him."*

John 14:23-24 *Jesus answered him, "If anyone loves me, he will keep my word, and my Father will love him, and we will come to him and make our home with him. Whoever does not love me does not keep my words. And the word that you hear is not mine but the Father's, who sent me."*

So, Jesus himself says the words He speaks and the commandments He follows are those of his Father, not his own. He also states if you love him you will keep his commandments, which are whose? — His Father's.

John 15:10 *If you keep my commandments, you will abide in my love, just as I have kept my Father's commandments and abide in his love.*

1 John 2:2-6 *He is the propitiation for our sins, and not for ours only but also for the sins of the whole world. And by this we know that we have come to know him, if we keep his commandments. Whoever says "I know him" but does not keep his commandments is a liar, and the truth is not in him, but whoever keeps his word, in him truly the love of God is perfected. By this we may know that we are in him: whoever says he abides in him ought to walk in the same way in which he walked.*

Full stop! Re-read this passage at least two more times. I would ask that you really think about this. Yeshua (Jesus) walked without sin. He followed the commandments of YHWH perfectly and didn't change or break them. ***And we are to walk in the same way in which He walked!*** We will cover what this means more in-depth in the next chapter.

1 John 5:3 *For this is the love of God, that we keep his commandments. And his commandments are not burdensome.*

2 John 1:6 *And this is love, that we walk according to his commandments; this is the commandment, just as you have heard from the beginning, so that you should walk in it.*

As you can see, the Bible does state unequivocally and undoubtedly how to love YHWH. The entirety of Psalms 119 talks about the love of YHWH and how to love Him. Loving Him as defined by the Bible is obeying the commandments of YHWH. Now, there is no way I could possibly mean obeying the commandments given to Moses, right?

Yes, that is what I mean. Now you have three choices: you can either close the book and give me a bad review based on just this paragraph; you can continue to read just so you can write a review, YouTube video or counter novel to prove me wrong; or you can continue to read, be open to what is written, and research it for yourself. Test it against the scriptures and love YHWH as HE tells you to. Please keep reminding yourself throughout this book and whenever you read your Bible that it was written not with a Western/Greek mindset, but with an Eastern/Hebrew mindset. At the time the Bible was written and the time the writers lived, they were in eastern culture, and there was only one testament. The law, writings, and prophets in the Old Testament were all they had. So, when the Apostles in the New Testament refer to "the scriptures" or state something about them, they are talking about the Torah, writings, and prophets before Matthew. I am in no way dismissing the New Testament. What I am saying is the New Testament confirms and compliments the Old Testament instead of eradicating it as we have been taught.

Go back to the first paragraph in this chapter. We talked about the love languages book. Say you read the book with your spouse. You learned your love languages and theirs, and the odds are you both had separate ones. How do you think you would feel if your spouse knew your love language but decided to ignore it and love you only how they wanted to? Wasn't the premise of the book to learn how to love your partner in the way they want you to? How would they feel if your love language was expressed as acts of servitude and theirs with gifts and you never gave gifts, but instead always did things for them? Yes, they may feel it's nice, but it is not speaking to their hearts. You are ignoring how they want to be loved for your own understanding. It isn't our understanding but THEIRS that matters. So, keep this in mind the next time you are praying over your pork chops and thanking YHWH for them.

Proverbs 3:5-6 *Trust in the LORD with all thine heart; and lean not unto thine own understanding. In all thy ways acknowledge him, and he shall direct thy paths.*

By now you are probably on your computer writing me a scathing email calling me a heretic. Before you hit send, re-read that verse from Proverbs. Whose understanding are you leaning on? We are to lean on the scriptures to tell us how to understand. Your minister was taught the same things he is teaching you. And there are many videos about how seminary school no longer focuses on the scriptures but on growing the church and running it like a business. Yes, these leaders put a lot of time and effort into their education. But what are they being taught? When you are first saved and baptized, you were probably given a Bible or booklet telling you where to start. For me it was Romans—Romans road to salvation. For some it is John. Why are we never taught to start at

Genesis? The Bible and school textbooks are the only books you are ever told to skip parts and ignore others. Why? It all matters and applies. Reading the Old Testament won't change how you understand the New—will it?

If you were to give a Bible to the chieftain of a remote village understanding that he only knew the Bible was true and applicable today, a year later would the village remain unchanged? Remember that he knew nothing about dispensationalism or other theologies. He simply read and accepted the book as written. Would the village under his leadership keep eating what they had been eating, celebrate their own holy days as they had before? Would they do this with the understanding that it was not what the book stated, but that they would always be forgiven without changing any of their old ways? I believe in this situation, the village would be following the complete Torah as stated in the Bible. They would understand not only that Yeshua died for their sins, providing salvation, but that following the Torah was an act of love and obedience to Yeshua and YHWH. They would no longer be eating everything they wanted or celebrating false gods. They would be leaning not on their own understanding but what is stated and set forth in the scriptures.

But The Laws Were Abolished

Matthew 5:17 *"Do not think that I came to destroy the Law or the Prophets. I did not come to destroy but to fulfill."*

To properly counter this argument, we have to answer a fundamental question. What is sin? If you were to go into a church and ask a minister or believer what sin was, you may get a variety of different answers. Disobeying the ten commandments would probably be the most popular. Ironic as that would be, because you would find the churchgoers there on a Sunday. Sunday is not the Sabbath. "Remember my Sabbath and keep it holy." But that is for another chapter. How does the Bible define sin?

1 John 3:4 *Whosoever committeth sin transgresseth also the law: for sin is the transgression of the law.*

So, to transgress or break the Law is what the Bible defines as sin. In the first chapter, we covered what Yeshua said in John 14:23-34. Yeshua said, *"And the word that you hear is not mine but the Father's, who sent me."* So, why is it we're taught that He came to completely destroy and change what His Father says to do?

Also, consider this paradox. If Yeshua did away with the law, then He did away with sin, because sin defined by the Bible is a transgression of the law. And if He did away with sin, then there is no need for salvation. Stick with me on this. We are taught that Yeshua came to fulfill the law. He says it right there in Matthew 5:17-18. We're taught that we no longer have to obey the law, because they are just too hard; or because we aren't Jewish, they do not apply to us; or my favorite, because Yeshua walked it out perfectly, so we don't have to. So, to most modern Christians, Matthew 5:17-18 says, "Do not think that I came to destroy the Law or the Prophets. I did not come to destroy but to destroy." Say what now? That makes no sense at all. Fulfill doesn't mean to destroy, abolish, or do away with.

If you think I am wrong, let's look at other times fulfill is used in scripture. For the sake of argument, I will quote the original then put destroy in the place of fulfill to see if it makes sense. You will find it completely changes the context of the scripture.

Matthew 3:15 But Jesus answered and said to him, "Permit it to be so now, for thus it is fitting for us to fulfill all righteousness." Then he allowed Him.

Modern understanding of fulfill: But Jesus answered and said to him, "Permit it to be so now, for thus it is fitting for us to destroy all righteousness." Then he allowed Him.

Exodus 23:26 "No one shall suffer miscarriage or be barren in your land; I will fulfill the number of your days.

Modern understanding of fulfill: "No one shall suffer miscarriage or be barren in your land; I will destroy the number of your days."

Psalm 20:4 May He grant you according to your heart's desire and fulfill all your purpose.

17

Modern understanding of fulfill: May He grant you according to your heart's desire AND destroy all your purpose.

CHALLENGE TIME: To drive this point home a little more, try it for yourself. Go to www.blueletterbible.org or any favorite Bible study website with a word search option, and type in the word, "fulfill" into the search engine. Get a sheet of paper and rewrite them replacing fulfill with destroy, do away with, or abolish.

Whoa! That changes YHWH and Yeshua from loving and benevolent to destructive and sadistic. In fact, it doesn't sound like them at all but the enemy, HaSatan (Satan). With your new understanding of the word, "fulfill," you must conclude that Yeshua didn't come to destroy the Laws. So, what could He have meant by this? Let's look at the context of the passages I used. Whenever the word, "fulfill" was used, it was to bring it to its best and fullest possibility. We could say that Yeshua did not come to destroy the law, but to bring it to the best, fullest possibility, and understanding.

Imagine having an above ground swimming

pool. The kind that gets bigger and steadier once it is filled to the line with water. You get the pool out of the box, hook up your hose and, "get to waiting". Now imagine your children whining to get in already. The sun is beating down on you. Your patience is wearing thin, and FINALLY, after what seems forever, the pool is filled to the line. It has become, "fulfilled." Now that it has met its best potential, do you take it right back down and throw the pool away? NO! You and your children would jump in and enjoy the water. How disappointed would you feel if your children said they wouldn't use the pool because it was too full?

Matthew 5:18 *"For assuredly, I say to you, till heaven and earth pass away, one jot or one tittle will by no means pass from the law till all is fulfilled."*

HAHA! Now you think you have me in a corner with this verse. I just explained what fulfilled meant. Yeshua said He came to fulfill the law, and this scripture states that when all is fulfilled, the law will be done away with. I ask you to reread this and Matthew 5:17. What is the key phrase in this scripture that is often glossed over? — "Till all is fulfilled." What did Yeshua mean by, "ALL?" He means the prophets. He spoke of them in verse seventeen and readdressed it in eighteen. So, the law will not be abolished until the law and prophets are brought to their best and fullest understanding.

Anyone who is a believer on any level knows and understands that not all the prophecies of the Bible have come true yet, and not all the prophecies are completely understood. It is still speculation and educated guessing. And until Yeshua comes, that is all it will be. With our new found understanding, the only logical conclusion is that the law is not done away with.

There are some who hold the belief that only two laws need to be followed; love the Lord with all your heart and love your neighbor. There are yet still some who believe that only the ten commandments apply. I would say both are correct and incorrect. The two commandments as stated by Yeshua are condensed explanations of the better known ten commandments. If you look at the ten commandments, the first four speak of how to love and worship YHWH, and the last six tell you how to love your neighbor. But if you read the Bible as it is meant to be read from the first page, you would understand that the ten commandments are the cliffnotes of the Torah. There is a wonderful website that explains this in more detail, *www.the613.info*.

"But," you say, "Romans chapter ten says that the law of righteousness has ended." I have to admit this stumped me at first. Right there it says, "ended." That is pretty clear and doesn't leave a lot of wiggle room in English. Oh, Paul, the most misunderstood and misinterpreted man in the Bible. I believe he is the reason behind the saying, "It's all Greek to me!"

Paul's writings are arguably the only scriptures in the Bible that come with their own warning label. Peter warned readers not to misunderstand Paul's writings. If not understood in context, they could twist them to fit their own doctrines and beliefs and lead you into lawlessness.

***2 Peter 3:14-18** So then, dear friends, since you are looking forward to this, make every effort to be found spotless, blameless and at peace with him. Bear in mind that our Lord's patience means salvation, just as our dear brother Paul also wrote* *you with the wisdom that God gave him. He writes the same way in all his letters, speaking in them of these matters. His letters contain some things that are hard to understand, which ignorant and unstable people distort, as they do the other Scriptures, to their own destruction. Therefore, dear friends, since you have been forewarned, be on your guard so that you may not be carried away by the error of the lawless and fall from your secure position. But grow in the grace and knowledge of our Lord and Savior Jesus Christ. To him be glory both now and forever! Amen.*

Romans 10:3-4 *For they being ignorant of God's righteousness, and going about to establish their own righteousness, have not submitted themselves unto the righteousness of God. For Christ is the end of the law for righteousness to everyone that believeth.*

Strong's Definition of end: τέλος télos, tel'-os; from a primary τέλλω téllō (to set out for a definite point or goal); properly, the point aimed at as a limit *Strong's Exhaustive Concordance: King James Version Bible* Updated ed. La Habra:Lockman Foundation, 1995.

https://biblehub.com/greek/5056.htm / (hereafter cited in text as *Strong's*).

So, is Christ the end or the goal of the law of righteousness? We should determine what the biblical definition of righteousness is first.

Deuteronomy 6:25 *And it shall be our righteousness, if we observe to do all these commandments before the LORD our God, as he hath commanded us.*

Remember Yeshua Himself said that He did not come to abolish the law but to fulfill it. So, if Paul was stating that Christ was the end of the law of righteousness, then he would be directly contradicting the Messiah himself and should be thrown out of the Bible and labeled a heretic. Since that is not the case, let us come to the understanding of the context.

Romans 10:3-4 *For they being ignorant of God's righteousness* (observing and following the commandments of YHWH)*, and going about to establish their own righteousness,* (NOT observing and following the commandments of YHWH) *have* *not submitted themselves unto the righteousness of God. For Christ is the end*(goal) *of the law for righteousness (*observing and following the commandments of YHWH*) to everyone that believeth.*

Paul is saying Yeshua is our goal in how we are to observe and follow the laws of YHWH. As my teenage daughter would say, "He is goals."

Acts 24:14 *But this I confess unto thee, that after the way which they call heresy, so worship I the God of my fathers, believing all things which are written in the law and in the prophets:*

Okay, but the Torah was nailed to the cross.

Colossians 2:13-14 *And you, who were dead in your trespasses and the uncircumcision of your flesh, God made alive together with him, having forgiven us all our trespasses, by canceling the record of debt that stood against us with its legal demands. This he set aside, nailing it to the cross.*

Once again, Paul is being misinterpreted for lawlessness! We will cover more of the misuse of Paul's writings in a later chapter. But for now, we

24

will just cover the last scripture and this one. This phrase itself aggravates my soul. I think because people tend to say it so dismissively, tossing it out there as if it wasn't a big deal, just a small thing Yeshua did for us. Was the Torah nailed to the cross? —Absolutely and thankfully so!

John 1:14 And the Word became flesh and dwelt among us, and we have seen his glory, glory as of the only Son, from the Father, full of grace and truth.

Yeshua was the Torah made flesh.

So, what was being blotted out as stated in Colossians? Let's look at the law and what it's referring to.

Numbers 5:11-23 And the Lord spoke to Moses, saying, "Speak to the people of Israel, If any man's wife goes astray and breaks faith with him, if a man lies with her sexually, and it is hidden from the eyes of her husband, and she is undetected though she has defiled herself, and there is no witness against her, since she was not taken in the act, and if the spirit of jealousy comes over him and he is jealous

*of his wife who has defiled herself, or if the spirit of
jealousy comes over him and he is jealous of his
wife, though she has not defiled herself, then the
man shall bring his wife to the priest and bring the
offering required of her, a tenth of an ephah of
barley flour. He shall pour no oil on it and put no
frankincense on it, for it is a grain offering of
jealousy, a grain offering of remembrance, bringing
iniquity to remembrance. And the priest shall bring
her near and set her before the Lord. And the priest
shall take holy water in an earthenware vessel and
take some of the dust that is on the floor of the
tabernacle and put it into the water. And the priest
shall set the woman before the Lord and unbind the
hair of the woman's head and place in her hands the
grain offering of remembrance, which is the grain
offering of jealousy. And in his hand the priest shall
have the water of bitterness that brings the curse.
Then the priest shall make her take an oath, saying,
'If no man has lain with you, and if you have not
turned aside to uncleanness while you were under
your husband's authority, be free from this water of
bitterness that brings the curse. But if you have
gone astray, though you are under your husband's
authority, and if you have defiled yourself, and*

some man other than your husband has lain with you, then' (let the priest make the woman take the oath of the curse, and say to the woman) 'the Lord make you a curse and an oath among your people, when the Lord makes your thigh fall away and your body swell. May this water that brings the curse pass into your bowels and make your womb swell and your thigh fall away.' And the woman shall say, 'Amen, Amen.' Then the priest shall write these curses in a book and wash them off into the water of bitterness.

John 19:28-30 *After this, Jesus knowing that all things were now accomplished, that the scripture might be fulfilled, saith, I thirst. Now there was set a vessel full of vinegar: and they filled a sponge with vinegar, (bitter water) and put it upon hyssop, and put it to his mouth. When Jesus therefore had received the vinegar, he said, It is finished: and he bowed his head, and gave up the ghost.*

Yeshua had to fulfill all the scriptures. In John nineteen, we see that He was blotting out the sins of Israel (the adulterous woman), fulfilling the scriptures in Numbers. When He said "it is finished," He was saying He met all the requirements, fulfilling the scriptures that made Him the foretold Messiah. Our (Israel) sin of adultery had to be blotted out. He took the punishment for our sin of adultery as described in Jeremiah three and laid forth as law in Numbers chapter five.

Numbers 5:21 *the Lord make you a curse and an oath among your people* (cause your people to curse and denounce you).

Matthew 27:39 *And they that passed by reviled him, wagging their heads,*

Again, fulfilling the scriptures and walking them out without error.

The living Torah was also beaten, spit upon, humiliated, verbally abused, and ultimately suffered a horrible death on that cross.

Matthew 27:28-31 28 *And they stripped him and put a scarlet robe on him, and twisting together a crown of thorns, they put it on his head and put a reed in his right hand. And kneeling before him, they mocked him, saying, "Hail, King of the Jews!" And they spit on him and took the reed and struck*

him on the head. And when they had mocked him,
they stripped him of the robe and put his own
clothes on him and led him away to crucify him.

But what most people overlook is that the same
Torah went through hell:

__1 Peter 3:19-20__ After being made alive, he went
and made proclamation to the imprisoned spirits—
to those who were disobedient long ago when God
waited patiently in the days of Noah while the ark
was being built...

Conquered death:

__2 Timothy 2:10 10__ and which now has been
manifested through the appearing of our Savior
Christ Jesus, who abolished death and brought life
and immortality to light through the gospel,

AND ROSE AGAIN! AMEN!

__John 20:11-16__ Now Mary stood outside the
tomb crying. As she wept, she bent over to look into
the tomb and saw two angels in white, seated where
Jesus' body had been, one at the head and the other
at the foot. They asked her, "Woman, why are you

crying?" "They have taken my Lord away," she
said, "and I don't know where they have put him."
At this, she turned around and saw Jesus standing
there, but she did not realize that it was Jesus. He
asked her, "Woman, why are you crying? Who is it
you are looking for?" Thinking he was the
gardener, she said, "Sir, if you have carried him
away, tell me where you have put him, and I will get
him." Jesus said to her, "Mary."

Yes, the Torah was nailed to the cross, but it did
not end there. He lives still and is coming back for
us. Praise YHWH and Yeshua! And the next time
you hear someone blithely say, "Well, the Torah
was nailed to the cross," think about what that really
means and maybe explain to them how they
shouldn't take it so lightly and view it with a little
more reverence.

WE ARE GENTILES...RIGHT?

Ephesians 2:18-19 *For through him we both have access in one Spirit to the Father. So, then you are no longer strangers and aliens, but you are fellow citizens with the saints and members of the household of God*

I have family members who have both adopted and biological children. If you were to watch them together as a family, you would never know which child was biological and which was not. They do not treat the children any differently. The same love, rules, and expectations are for all. In the beginning, as the adopted children got used to their new home, they may have had a small bit of grace so they could acclimate to their new family. Now years later, they aren't treated any different, because they know better. They are now grafted into the family and expected to behave as such.

When you start going to church, it is often taught that we are Gentiles, that we the church are separate from Israel—the special kids that YHWH decided to have as His new favorites. And because we are His new favorites, we get special privileges and rights the other guys don't, as if YHWH were that petty and superficial! If you look at the Strong's definition of the word, "Gentile," you may start to see that being called a Gentile when you are a believer in Yeshua could actually be interpreted an insult.

Strong's Definitions of Gentile ἔθνος éthnos, eth'-nos; probably from G1486; a race (as of the same habit), i.e. a tribe; specially, a foreign (non-Jewish) one (usually, by implication, pagan): — Gentile, heathen, nation, people. (*Strong's G1484*)

1 Peter 2:11 Keep your conduct among the Gentiles honorable, so that when they speak against you as evildoers, they may see your good deeds and glorify God on the day of visitation.

If we were still considered Gentiles, then why would Peter make it a point to tell us to act differently from them, to keep our conduct honorable? Why would there need to be a distinction if we are Gentiles too?

Are you a Pagan? Are you a heathen? Do you not belong to YHWH's nation? I would hope the answers are no, no, and yes. We will assume you did and continue. You and I are not Gentile Christians. We are not a separate church. WE ARE ISRAEL! We are grafted in, just like my adopted family members.

Acts 7:38 *This is he, that was in the church in the wilderness with the angel which spake to him in the mount Sinai, and with our fathers: who received the lively oracles to give unto us:*

If the church was a separate entity from Israel, why does Stephen reference Yeshua as being in the church in the wilderness with the angels and their fathers (Hebrews of the Exodus) at Mt. Sinai? The Hebrews and the Greeks understood that church meant congregation or assembly, nothing more. Modern day churches tend to lead their followers to assume that the church is separate or an unspoken thirteenth tribe. When you accept Yeshua as your savior, you agree to join Israel and all its statutes

33

and rules.

Numbers 15:15-16 One ordinance shall be both for you of the congregation, and also for the stranger that sojourneth with you, an ordinance forever in your generations: as ye are, so shall the stranger be before the LORD. One law and one manner shall be for you, and for the stranger that sojourneth with you.

Galatians 3:28 There is neither Jew nor Greek, there is neither bond nor free, there is neither male nor female: for ye are all one in Christ Jesus.

Romans 10:12-13 For there is no difference between the Jew and the Greek: for the same Lord over all is rich unto all that call upon him. For whosoever shall call upon the name of the Lord shall be saved.

These versus, right here in the Old and New Testaments, state that we are no different from one another. Only Israel and Judah would be the favorite children. Everyone who chooses Yeshua and follows His commandments are a part of it! In fact, had it not been for Gentiles or foreigners being allowed to be grafted in, we would not have Yeshua at all. Ruth and Rahab (the prostitute in Jericho) were both grafted into Israel and are in the direct lineage of Yeshua as outlined in Matthew 1:5. Isn't that wonderful? Not only were these two women allowed to be grafted into YHWH's kingdom, their lineages were picked to be the one of our Savior! This proves that it doesn't matter what you are born into; it is who you are REBORN into.

Romans 9:6-8 *Not as though the word of God hath taken none effect. For they are not all Israel, which are of Israel: Neither, because they are the seed of Abraham, are they all children: but, In Isaac shall thy seed be called That is, they which are the children of the flesh, these are not the children of God: but the children of the promise are counted for the seed.*

1 Peter 2:9-10 *But you are a chosen race, a royal priesthood, a holy nation, a people for his own possession, that you may proclaim the excellencies of him who called you out of darkness into his marvelous light. Once you were not a people, but now you are God's people; once you had not received mercy, but now you have received* *mercy.*

Peter is telling you who you are in these verses, YHWH's chosen people. The first three-fourths of the book was describing how the Hebrews (Israel and Judah) were His chosen people, and that He would divorce Israel and scatter her among the nations and then get her back. Why would the last part of the book change this? If that were the case, then why have the first portion of the book at all?

Romans 11:23-24 *And even they, if they do not continue in their unbelief, will be grafted in, for God has the power to graft them in again. For if you were cut from what is by nature a wild olive tree, and grafted, contrary to nature, into a cultivated olive tree, how much more will these, the natural branches, be grafted back into their own olive tree...*

Now I am not an Arborist, but to successfully graft branches into a tree, they need to be similar. They need to work with each other so the branch will seamlessly grow into the established tree. If something goes wrong, it will put the whole tree in danger. The branch has to follow the terms that the tree has established. We may be the grafted in wild branches or even cut away natural ones, but to stay on the tree, we have to calm down and live by the tree's rules.

Galatians 3:7-8 *Know then that it is those of faith who are the sons of Abraham. And the scripture, foreseeing that God would justify the heathen through faith, preached before the gospel unto Abraham, saying, In thee shall all nations be blessed.*

Ephesians 2:11-13 *Wherefore remember, that ye being in time past Gentiles in the flesh, who are called Uncircumcision by that which is called the Circumcision in the flesh made by hands; That at that time ye were without Christ, being aliens from the commonwealth of Israel, and strangers from the covenants of promise, having no hope, and without God in the world: But now in Christ Jesus ye who sometimes were far off are made nigh by the blood of Christ.*

Colossians 3:15 *And let the peace of Christ rule in your hearts, to which indeed you were called in one body. And be thankful.*

If we are separate from Israel or Judah, then
where are we mentioned in the book of Revelation?
The Gentile church is not mentioned in any form in
the book of Revelation. If you are thinking "The
church of Philadelphia," or the one hundred and
forty-four thousand, then rethink it. There are over
forty thousand denominations with millions of
members that all say or think the same thing. Isn't it
more logical that the ten missing tribes of Israel and
the tribe of Judah are the followers referred to in
Revelation? If there are twelve total tribes, then the
one hundred and forty-four thousand could be
twelve thousand from each tribe, elected by
YHWH. The Bible repeatedly warns not to add to
scripture. Yet the church adds, morphs, and
misinterprets it constantly. For more information on
that look up the *Error of Dispensationalism* and
Identity Crisis on YouTube.

Matthew 15:24 *He answered, "I was sent only
to the lost sheep of the house of Israel."*

We're grafted into Israel, thankfully, to the
Kingdom by YHWH's never-ending grace and
goodness. But, because Israel was scattered
throughout the nations and adopted their traditions,

beliefs, and gods, and Israel played the whore, we do not know where the tribes went or what tribe we would originally belong to, if any. But because we are grafted in, we do know that we are to obey the laws of the Kingdom, because we belong there.

But What About The New Covenant?

Jeremiah 31:31 Behold, the days are coming, declares the LORD, when I will make a new covenant with the house of Israel and the house of Judah,

A covenant is a contract or agreement involving two or more parties.

One of my favorite YouTube channel hosts, Zachary Baur from *New2Torah*, has a great analogy I thought I would share.

When you sign a lease agreement for an apartment, you sign a contract stating that you will obey the rules that they state. In return, they will provide you with a place to live, maintenance, etc. This agreement states that you will only place trash in allowed places. You will not have a pet, and you will not play loud music after ten at night. You decide to throw your trash where ever you want, get a Siberian husky, and blast your music after 10 p.m. You're evicted. Now that you're evicted, someone else wants to move in. They enter into a new covenant! Will the covenant terms change for this new person? No, they will not.

There isn't a whole lot specifically on a scripturally backed understanding of the new covenant. But there is an article I read during my research. I won't mention the name for the simple fact it says the old covenant was flawed as its argument for support of the new covenant. Stating that any part of the Bible or His laws are flawed is stating that He was wrong and thus fallible.

Proverbs 30:5 *Every word of God proves true; he is a shield to those who take refuge in*

Psalms 18:30 *As for God, his way is perfect: the word of the LORD is tried: he is a buckler to all those that trust in him.*

Now the whole chapter of Jeremiah thirty-one speaks about the new covenant, but only a few verses directly mention it.

Take a look at the scripture that mentions the ew covenant in its entirety.

Jeremiah 31:31-33 *Behold, the days come, saith the LORD, that I will make a new covenant with the house of Israel, and with the house of Judah: Not according to the covenant that I made with their fathers in the day that I took them by the hand to bring them out of the land of Egypt; which my covenant they break, although I was an husband unto them, saith the LORD: But this shall be the covenant that I will make with the house of Israel; After those days, saith the LORD, I will put my law in their inward parts, and write it in their hearts; and will be their God, and they shall be my people. And they shall teach no more every man his neighbour, and every man his brother, saying, Know the LORD: for they shall all know me, from the least of them unto the greatest of them, saith the LORD: for I will forgive their iniquity, and I will remember their sin no more.*

So, let's review the first line. Most Christians will deny being a part of the House of Israel or the

House of Judah. This new covenant is meant for them. It says so right there, *"Behold, the days come, saith the LORD, that I will make a new covenant with the house of Israel, and with the house of Judah."* It doesn't say Judah, Israel, and the Gentiles. This reinforces what we learned in the previous chapter.

It says, *"I will put the LAW on their inward parts and write it in their hearts."* Is the law written in every believer's heart yet? If that were so, then you wouldn't be reading this right now. No one automatically knows the laws or how they are to be followed. Nor do they know what the clear-cut holy days' actual dates are or how to observe them as soon as they accept Yeshua as their savior.

So why is He going to make a new covenant with Israel and Judah that promises to write the law on their hearts only for it to be irrelevant and no longer apply? This makes as much sense as wiping yourself before you go to the restroom.

Now let's look at the other part of the covenant. *"And they shall teach no more every man his neighbour and every man his brother, saying Know the LORD: for they shall all know me."* Has this happened yet? Thousands of missionaries spreading the gospel across the world would say no. I could also argue the mere fact that there are millions of churches spanning the globe is a vote for no as well.

Even if we are in a new covenant, it doesn't say it abolishes the law; it states the opposite. Even if you were to search in the previous verses, you would only prove the point more so. For example:

Jeremiah 31:27-28 *"Behold, the days are coming, declares the LORD, when I will sow the house of Israel and the house of Judah with the seed of man and the seed of beast. And it shall come to pass that as I have watched over them to pluck up and break down, to overthrow, destroy, and bring harm, so I will watch over them to build and to plant, declares the LORD.*

Most everyone agrees this verse is referring to the physical country of Israel being reinstated by YHWH to full power and glory as stated in the scriptures. Yet, if you really think about this, then you would know this is not true. (Stop calling me antisemitic long enough to read why.)

Current Israel, though it may have been brought together by YHWH, does not observe the laws of Torah as YHWH commanded them. If they did, they would not have one of the world's largest week-long gay pride celebrations every year. They also deny the Messiah. If the new covenant is completed because of Yeshua, wouldn't it make sense that the new Israel would accept him? In fact, in order for you to be a citizen of Israel, you must deny Yeshua as Messiah unless you are a blood descendant of a Jew. They are not the House of Israel, yet. Both Judah and Israel (the people) spoken of in the new covenant will have to meet all the terms outlined in the new covenant to be the House of Israel once again. Both must follow the Torah as it is intended to be followed and accept Yeshua as Messiah.

The New Covenant re-enforces that the law still applies.

Jeremiah 31:35-37 *Thus saith the LORD, which giveth the sun for a light by day, and the ordinances of the moon and of the stars for a light by night, which divideth the sea when the waves thereof roar; The LORD of hosts is his name: If those ordinances*

46

depart from before me, saith the LORD, then the seed of Israel also shall cease from being a nation before me forever. Thus saith the LORD; If heaven above can be measured, and the foundations of the earth searched out beneath, I will also cast off all the seed of Israel for all that they have done, saith the LORD.

What is the definition of an ordinance? **Strong's Definition חֹק chôq,** khoke; from H2710; an enactment; hence, an appointment (of time, space, quantity, labor or usage): —appointed, bound, commandment, convenient, custom, decree(-d), due, law, measure, × necessary, ordinance(-nary), portion, set time, statute, task. (*Strongs H2708*).

Since YHWH stated that He would make a new covenant with Israel placing the law on their hearts, it can be determined that the law will never be done away with. The ordinances of the sun, moon, and stars are still here. Heaven has never been measured, and we haven't been able to crack more than eight miles below the crust of the Earth to determine its foundation to search it out. According to His own words these things must happen before, and are the only way, He will forever turn Israel away. We are not under the new covenant yet. This will happen at the marriage supper.

Revelation 19:6-10 *Then I heard what seemed to be the voice of a great multitude, like the roar of many waters and like the sound of mighty peals of thunder, crying out, "Hallelujah! For the Lord our God, the Almighty reigns. Let us rejoice and exult and give him the glory, for the marriage of the Lamb has come, and his Bride has made herself ready; it was granted her to clothe herself with fine linen, bright and pure"— for the fine linen is the righteous deeds of the saints. And the angel said to me, "Write this: Blessed are those who are invited to the marriage supper of the Lamb." And he said to me, "These are the true words of God."*

BUT THE LAW WAS MADE TOO HARD

__Deuteronomy 30:11-12__ Now what I am commanding you today is not too difficult for you or beyond your reach. It is not up in heaven, so that you have to ask, "Who will ascend into heaven to get it and proclaim it to us so we may obey it?"

When you are in church, you are told the law is too hard. It's a burden, a yoke too heavy to bear. They simply cannot be kept. We're told it was so hard that Jesus had to come down to rescue us from it; so difficult no one could follow it. Are we not made in the image of YHWH? Does He make mistakes? We are never taught the verses in context or those that state the contrary. So, in this chapter I am just going to list many verses that state otherwise.

Proverbs 6:23 *For the commandment is a lamp, and the law is light, and reproofs of instruction are the way of life:*

Proverbs 28:7 *Whoso keepeth the law is a wise son: but he that is a companion of riotous men shameth his father.*

Romans 7:12 *Wherefore the law is holy, and the commandment holy, and just, and good.*

1 John 5:3 *For this is the love of God, that we keep his commandments: and his commandments are not grievous.*

Proverbs 4:2 *For I give you good doctrine, forsake ye not my law.*

1 Timothy 1:8 *But we know that the law is good, if a man use it lawfully;*

Job 23:12 *I have not departed from the commandment of his lips; I have treasured the words of his mouth more than my portion of food.*

Psalm 112:1 *Praise the LORD! Blessed is the man who fears the LORD, who greatly delights in his commandments!*

Psalm 119:1 ALEPH. Blessed are the undefiled in the way, who walk in the law of the LORD.

Psalm 119:2 *Blessed are they that keep his testimonies, and that seek him with the whole heart.*

Psalm 119:3 *They also do no iniquity: they walk in his ways.*

Psalm 119:4 *Thou hast commanded us to keep thy precepts diligently.*

Psalm 119:5_*O that my ways were directed to keep thy statutes!*

Psalm 119:6 *Then shall I not be ashamed, when I have respect unto all thy commandments.*

Psalm 119:7 *I will praise thee with uprightness of heart, when I shall have learned thy righteous judgments.*

Psalm 119:8 *I will keep thy statutes: O forsake me not utterly.*

Psalms 119:142 *Your righteousness is righteous forever, your law is true.*

Amos 5:17 *But let justice roll on like a river,*

righteousness like a never-failing stream!

And Lastly **Philippians 4:13** *I can do all things through Christ which strengtheneth me.*

If we can do all things through Yeshua, how can *anything,* including the laws found in the Torah, be too hard? We do not follow the law for salvation. We follow them because we love HIM. Yeshua's blood atones and washes our sins away. But you have to repent and not repeat. Our hearts are no longer stone, but flesh. The law is not too hard! Obeying the law makes it a more personal relationship with YHWH, not one between Him and the Nation, but one with only you and Him. Both are speaking each other's love languages.

BUT PAUL SAID...

As I mentioned earlier, Paul is the most misquoted and misunderstood contributors to the Bible. Some people want him completely removed from the Bible, claiming he is a heretic and goes against the Torah and other teachings. Others seem to be what I have called Paulonites. They cling to the misinterpretation of his word like Rose clung to that door in *Titanic*, using it as the be all, end all of the explanations about why the law no longer applies. Hopefully, in this chapter I will not only explain that Paul belongs in the Bible, but that he was a devout follower of Yeshua and loved the laws of YHWH.

When you read Paul, you have to remember he was a master of the Torah. He studied all his life and understood it. He spoke of at least four different laws: the Torah, the oral laws of the Jews, the law of Rome, or the curse of the law, (the punishments for breaking law being death)—the punishment Yeshua took for us. He wouldn't speak against the Torah or not follow it. You must look at whom he was writing to and know Torah to figure out which law he was talking about.

Galatians 3:24-25 *Wherefore the law was our schoolmaster to bring us unto Christ, that we might be justified by faith. But after that faith is come, we are no longer under a schoolmaster.*

Now, I don't understand how people can say this makes clear the law is done away with. But let's look at it. When you are in school, you are under a schoolmaster, a teacher, a tutor, whatever title you choose. They guide you and impart knowledge to you that lasts throughout your school career, hopefully. When you graduated did you forget every ounce of information that you learned? Does one plus one stop equaling two? Does the periodic table no longer exist? Now I know most of us forgot Algebra, but the laws of math haven't changed even if how you go about getting the answer has. (Do not get me started on the failure of Common Core!) Do you not use most of the basic things you were taught in school? So, with common sense and understanding, we can dismiss that this scripture proves the law is gone.

Did Paul teach against the law of circumcision? Did he teach that those who follow the Torah are under a curse? In the opening letter to Galatia, Paul says,

Galatians 1:6-9 *I marvel that ye are so soon removed from him that called you into the grace of Christ unto another gospel: Which is not another; but there be some that trouble you, and would pervert the gospel of Christ. But though we, or an angel from heaven, preach any other gospel unto you than that which we have preached unto you, let him be accursed. As we said before, so say I now again, If any man preach any other gospel unto you than that ye have received, let him be accursed.*

I will answer the second question first. Did he teach that those who follow the Torah are cursed because it is against the Gospel of Christ? No, he did not. Remember, Yeshua himself said that His commandments were his Father's. He is the Torah made flesh and walked it out perfectly so that we would have a goal, an example of how to worship and love YHWH. In the verse, Paul is actually quoting from Deuteronomy thirteen.

Deuteronomy 13:1-5 *If there arise among you a prophet, or a dreamer of dreams, and giveth thee a sign or a wonder, And the sign or the wonder come to pass, whereof he spake unto thee, saying, Let us go after other gods, which thou hast not known, and let us serve them; Thou shalt not hearken into the words of that prophet, or that dreamer of dreams: for the LORD your God proveth you, to know whether ye love the LORD your God with all your heart and with all your soul. Ye shall walk after the LORD your God, and fear him, and keep his commandments, and obey his voice, and ye shall serve him, and cleave unto him. And that prophet, or that dreamer of dreams, shall be put to death; because he hath spoken to turn you away from the LORD your God, which brought you out of the land of Egypt, and redeemed you out of the house of bondage, to thrust thee out of the way which the LORD thy God commanded thee to walk in. So shalt thou put the evil away from the midst of thee.*

He wrote this because there were believers in

Galatia that were mixing Pagan traditions with the worship of YHWH.

Galatians 4:8-9 *Formerly, when you did not know God, you were enslaved to those that by nature are not gods. But now that you have come to know God, or rather to be known by God, how can you turn back again to the weak and worthless elementary principles of the world, whose slaves you want to be once more?*

There were also those who followed the Torah, but were teaching that you had to have a circumcision before you could have salvation (works-based salvation).

Galatians 2:3-5 *But even Titus, who was with me, was not forced to be circumcised, though he was a Greek. Yet because of false brothers secretly brought in—who slipped in to spy out our freedom that we have in Christ Jesus, so that they might bring us into slavery—to them we did not yield in submission even for a moment, so that the truth of the gospel might be preserved for you.*

When Paul found out about this, he went to the

Jerusalem council to discuss it with John and the others. There were two circumcision groups: the one I mentioned earlier, and one that taught it was required after salvation and circumcision of the heart took place.

Act 15:7-11 And after there had been much debate, Peter stood up and said to them, "Brothers, you know that in the early days God made a choice among you, that by my mouth the Gentiles should hear the word of the gospel and believe. And God, who knows the heart, bore witness to them, by giving them the Holy Spirit just as he did to us, and he made no distinction between us and them, having cleansed their hearts by faith. Now, therefore, why are you putting God to the test by placing a yoke on the neck of the disciples that neither our fathers nor we have been able to bear? But we believe that we will be saved through the grace of the Lord Jesus, just as they will."

Peter was saying that works-based salvation is not possible (circumcision needed for salvation). Only salvation through faith is attainable. Because of salvation and the desire to obey YHWH in our hearts, the circumcision of the flesh will follow (complete compliance of YHWH's laws with heart, soul, flesh, and mind). Now you may think that this proves the law is too hard or not possible to follow. That is not what they are saying. We disproved that in the previous chapter. However, circumcision of the heart has to take place first, and that is in the Torah and the Prophets.

Deuteronomy 10:16 Circumcise therefore the foreskin of your heart, and be no longer stubborn.

Deuteronomy 30:6 And the LORD your God will circumcise your heart and the heart of your offspring, so that you will love the LORD your God with all your heart and with all your soul, that you may live.

Jeremiah 4:4 Circumcise yourselves to the LORD; remove the foreskin of your hearts, O men of Judah and inhabitants of Jerusalem; lest my wrath go forth like fire, and burn with none to quench it, because of the evil of your deeds."

Paul states this again in **Romans 7:22** *But a Jew is one inwardly, and circumcision is a matter of the heart, by the Spirit, not by the letter. His praise is* *not from man but from God.*

James also makes a decree in Acts 15:19-21 not to place hard expectations on new converts. The inward circumcision is what needs to be focused on first. Turning back to the practices and traditions of their former Pagan beliefs needs to be avoided. He addresses what all the Jews were taught as law in the synagogues weekly but was not taught in Pagan cities. Those practices that were against the Torah should be addressed and corrected first. Torah laws that were to focus on inward circumcision should be taught first and obedience to the rest would follow.

Acts 15:19-21 Therefore my judgment is that we should not trouble those of the Gentiles who turn to God, but should write to them to abstain from the things polluted by idols, and from sexual immorality, and from what has been strangled, and from blood. For from ancient generations Moses has had in every city those who proclaim him, for he is read every Sabbath in the synagogues. "

Look at Titus who is uncircumcised and Timothy who Paul met and circumcised after the Jerusalem council. If the council determined it wasn't important, why did Paul have Timothy circumcised, and why did Timothy allow it? I don't know too many men willing to put a sharp object near their most private parts, let alone allow someone to cut off a part of it for no reason other than a command from YHWH. Timothy was the son of a Jewish woman and a Greek man. He grew up hearing and knowing the ways and laws of YHWH. However, he wasn't circumcised, because it wasn't allowed by Jewish oral law. Timothy was already circumcised in his heart. Titus was a new convert, and although it wasn't stated, one can assume he was not fully circumcised in his heart, yet.

Does Paul say we can eat whatever we want, not have to celebrate the Old Testament holy days or observe the Sabbath? *sigh* No.

Colossians 2:16-17 *Let no man therefore judge you in meat, or in drink, or in respect of an holy day, or of the new moon, or of the sabbath days: Which are a shadow of things to come; but the body is of Christ.*

Paul says that food, drink, feasts, and holy days

are a shadow of things to come—a foreshadowing, which is a brief glimpse of what is going to come in full. In millennial reign, we will be celebrating the feasts and following the Torah fully with a joyful heart. For us to be a part of the body of Christ, we have to follow the shadow that is foretelling it. You can also look at it this way. A body casts a shadow, especially in bright light. The body of Christ's shadow is the Torah cast in the brightest light of all, YHWH.

Yeshua:

- died as the Passover Lamb (*Exodus 12:21-22*)

- was sinless (without leaven) at the beginning of the Feast of Unleavened Breads (*Exodus 12:15-17*)

- was resurrected as the first fruit on First Fruits (*Exodus 22:29*)

- and He poured out the cup on Pentecost for the Holy Spirit to teach and guide us in truth of the Torah (*John 14:15-27*)

He will come again to fulfill the fall feasts.

- He will return at the last trump on the Feast of Trumpets (*Leviticus 23:24, 1 Corinthians 15:52, Revelations 8:6*).

- He will judge the world on the Day of Atonement (*Leviticus 23:27, Revelations 20:11-15*).

- The Marriage Supper will take place on Sukkot/ The Feast of Tabernacles (*Leviticus 23:34, Revelations 6-9*).

- The Sabbath days are rest days. The Millennial reign is a thousand-year rest and fellowship with Messiah (*Exodus 20:11, Revelations 20:4*).

Also, remember that Yeshua picked Paul to go out to preach the gospel and convert Gentiles to the ways of YHWH. Paul traveled to Gentile nations, heathen nations that did not practice the Torah or recognize the laws. Those were to whom his letters were written, former Gentile converts. So, is Paul telling new converts not to worry about what their Pagan friends and families are saying about them observing the laws and holy days of the Torah? Or is he telling them that they should not be concerned about those who don't practice the Torah laws judging them about not observing the Torah laws? How would the Pagan Gentiles know to judge them? They wouldn't, because we are to be a set apart people, observing the set apart ways of the Father. This became a problem for the new converts. It is difficult for anyone to be outwardly different from everyone else.

Romans 15:18 For I will not venture to speak of anything except what Christ has accomplished through me to bring the Gentiles to obedience—by word and deed,

1 Corinthians 9:19-21 Though I am free of obligation to anyone, I make myself a slave to everyone, to win as many as possible. To the Jews I became like a Jew, to win the Jews. To those under the Law I became like one under the Law (though I myself am not under the Law), to win those under *the Law. To those without the Law I became like one without the Law (though I am not outside the law of God but am under the law of Christ), to win those without the Law....*

Again, I think this one is self-explanatory as well. It may not be to others. Paul is saying he is a free man. He made himself a servant to men, to minister to others. Notice in verse twenty and twenty-one, he made a discernment between being a Jew under the law (the laws Yeshua spoke against, the oral laws and traditions of man) and the law of God/Christ (John 7:16). He made a specific point to separate the difference between the two. He is also saying that to those wholly without the law (Gentile nations), he became like them. He probably adopted their slang and mannerisms, although he did not abandon the laws of God. Thus, he could convert them all back to the full Torah and ways of YHWH and righteousness.

Yeah, but Paul said in *Romans 6:14 For sin shall not have dominion over you: for ye are not under the law but under grace.*

For more context let's look at the previous verses:

*Romans 6:12-13 Let not sin (*break YHWH's commandments*) therefore reign in your mortal body, that ye should obey it in the lusts thereof.*

65

*Neither yield ye your members as instruments of unrighteousness (*not walking in YHWH's ways*) unto sin: (*breaking YHWH's commandments*) but yield yourselves unto God, as those that are alive from the dead, and your members as instruments of righteousness* (walking in YHWH's ways*) unto God.*

Paul is saying that because we have grace, we are no longer under the punishment of sin. We don't follow the law for salvation, which is impossible, but rather for correction, direction, and love of YHWH.

But he also said, **Romans 6:15** *What then? shall we sin, because we are not under the law, but under grace? God forbid.*

Paul was a proponent of the Laws of YHWH. He preached and followed them wherever he went, and to whomever he spoke. He stated it many times just in the book of Romans.

Romans 3:31 *Do we then make void the law through faith? God forbid: yea, we establish the law.*

Romans 7:12 *Wherefore the law is holy, and the commandment holy, and just, and good.*

Romans 7:22 *For I delight in the law of God after the inward man:*

Paul is misunderstood so much. Maybe now that there is a little more context and understanding to Paul, he can be better understood. When you start to get turned around or have a hard time understanding him, go back to the opening letter. See who he is talking to. Most importantly, remember Paul followed the Law of YHWH and understood the Torah better than most.

REPENTANCE IS A U-TURN

*Acts 26:20 but declared first to those in
Damascus, then in Jerusalem and throughout all the
region of Judea, and also to the Gentiles, that they
should repent and turn to God, performing deeds in
keeping with their repentance*

Having children, you learn a lot about repeated
mistakes, forgiveness, and repentance. Depending
on your parenting style, you may give your child
many warnings before you metaphorically put down
the hammer of justice. You may be a one and done
parent. You give one warning, and then they get
punished at the next transgression. Whatever way
you parent, you expect that once the forgiveness or
punishment has been given, they will not do the
offense again. If they commit it again, the
punishment may be more serious, and eventually
you as a parent start seeing the act as willful

defiance or rebellion. Depending on the age of your child, you may consider harsh or drastic means for correction. Military school or correction camps, and even in the worst cases juvenile detention or kicking them out of your home may be considered. However, the ultimate goal is that they will repent, change their ways, and decide to agree to your rules.

Revelations 3:19 *Those whom I love, I reprove and discipline, so be zealous and repent.*

Matthew 7:13-14 *Enter ye in at the strait gate: for wide is the gate, and broad is the way, that leadeth to destruction, and many there be which go in thereat: Because strait is the gate, and narrow is the way, which leadeth unto life, and few there be that find it.*

Many scriptures talk about repenting. When you are saved, you are told to repent of your sins and accept Yeshua as your savior. We have already used the scriptures to establish that sin is not obeying YHWH's laws as given to Moses and Abraham. Let's look at what it means to repent.

Strong's Definitions of repent μετανοέω
metanoéō, met-an-o-eh'-o; from G3326 and G3539;
to think differently or afterward, i.e. reconsider
(morally, feel compunction): —repent. (*Strong's
G3340*)

*1 Kings 8:47 yet if they turn their heart in the
land to which they have been carried captive, and
repent and plead with you in the land of their
captors, saying, 'We have sinned and have acted
perversely and wickedly,'*

*Psalm 7:12 If a man does not repent, God will
whet his sword; he has bent and readied his bow;*

*Ezekiel 18:30 Therefore I will judge you, O
house of Israel, every one according to his ways,
declares the Lord GOD. Repent and turn from all
your transgressions, lest iniquity be your ruin.*

"Repent" is mentioned over thirty-seven times
in the ESV, forty-six times in the KJV, and forty-six
times in the HNV (Hebrew Names Version). So,
you could say it is important.

*Revelations 2:4 But I have this against you, that
you have abandoned the love you had at first.*

Remember therefore from where you have fallen; repent, and do the works you did at first. If not, I will come to you and remove your lampstand from its place, unless you repent.

This is a great verse. It speaks specifically about the love of YHWH, and how we can return to it. What can be done to speak YHWH's love language? Do the works you did at first. What were the works? Following out the commandments.

Israel messed around and disobeyed YHWH for seven hundred years. He sent prophets and judges repeatedly warning her to stop what she was doing and come back to him. That is grace and patience I, as a parent or wife, will never understand or have. His love was so great for them that He watched them break the Torah and worship false gods for hundreds of years before He divorced her. The whole story of Hosea is about YHWH's efforts to bring Israel back. Over and over YHWH would say repent and come back to me, and they ignored the warnings and killed the messengers.

Jeremiah 3:8 *She saw that for all the adulteries of that faithless one, Israel, I had sent her away* *with a decree of divorce. Yet her treacherous sister Judah did not fear, but she too went and played the whore.*

Jeremiah 3:12 *Go and proclaim these words toward the north, and say, Return, thou backsliding Israel, saith the Lord; and I will not cause mine anger to fall upon you: for I am merciful, saith the Lord, and I will not keep anger forever.*

Now, you may ask, was Israel married to YHWH? In Exodus chapter nineteen, the first wedding of Israel took place. Before Israel and Judah were split into two houses, a covenant or a vow of faithfulness was exchanged between them.

Exodus 19:5-8 *Now therefore, if you will indeed obey my voice and keep my covenant, you shall be my treasured possession among all peoples, for all the earth is mine; and you shall be to me a kingdom of priests and a holy nation.' These are the words that you shall speak to the people of Israel." So Moses came and called the elders of the people and set before them all these words that the Lord had commanded him. All the people answered together and said, "All that the Lord has spoken we will do."*

73

And Moses reported the words of the people to the Lord. (These were essentially the 'I do's')

And Israel kept cheating, breaking the vows, and ultimately was cast out. This seems like a dilemma. If YHWH divorced Israel, and she went whoring after, how can He remarry her as He promised? Isn't that against His law?

Deuteronomy 24:1-4 *"When a man takes a wife and marries her, if then she finds no favor in his eyes because he has found some indecency in her, and he writes her a certificate of divorce and puts it in her hand and sends her out of his house, and she departs out of his house, and if she goes and becomes another man's wife, and the latter man hates her and writes her a certificate of divorce and puts it in her hand and sends her out of his house, or if the latter man dies, who took her to be his wife, then her former husband, who sent her away, may not take her again to be his wife, after she has been defiled, for that is an abomination before the Lord. And you shall not bring sin upon the land that the Lord your God is giving you for an inheritance.*

The only way Israel can repent and come back

to remarry YHWH as promised is for YHWH to die. Once someone has died, they are no longer under contractual obligation. And a woman can marry whomever she likes if she is a widow. Paul understood this and stated it when he said,

1 Corinthians 7:39 A wife is bound to her husband as long as he lives. But if her husband dies, she is free to be married to whom she wishes, only in the Lord.

And: Romans 7:1 Or do you not know, brothers —for I am speaking to those who know the law— that the law is binding on a person only as long as he lives?

So, because Yeshua came and died (remember He and His father are one), we as Israel can repent of our lawlessness, retake our vows, and commit to YHWH and His laws without breaking the Torah.

Anytime you come across the word, "repent" in the Bible, someone is either asking for forgiveness and wanting to turn back to the law, or being told to do so. My experience in the church or with most

Christians has been that they confuse repent and repeat. Of course, when we fall in the flesh, as we all do, we are forgiven, and Yeshua is an advocate for us in Heaven! But, to continually, knowingly, and willfully repeat sin is rebellion, and it is not covered by the blood of Yeshua.

1 John 2:1-6 My little children, I am writing these things to you so that you may not sin. But if anyone does sin, we have an advocate with the Father, Jesus Christ the righteous. He is the propitiation for our sins, and not for ours only but also for the sins of the whole world. And by this, we know that we have come to know him, if we keep his commandments. Whoever says "I know him" but does not keep his commandments is a liar, and the truth is not in him, but whoever keeps his word, in him truly the love of God is perfected. By this we may know that we are in him: whoever says he abides in him ought to walk in the same way in which he walked.

Hebrews 10:26-27 For if we go on sinning deliberately after receiving the knowledge of the truth, there no longer remains a sacrifice for sins, but a fearful expectation of judgment, and a fury of fire that will consume the adversaries.

Strongs Definition of rebellion *H5627* סָרָה
*carah revolt, rebellion, turn away, wrong, continual
stroke H6588* פֶּשַׁע *pesha` transgression, trespass,
sin, rebellion (Strong's H5627)*

The idea passively taught that repeated sin is
covered and forgiven is false and will lead you
down the road to destruction. If the road to
destruction is broad, you must repent and make a u-
turn back to the narrow path.

For a little more perspective, consider this. If
your spouse cheated once or twice, you *might*
forgive them and work it out together. Or as I
covered in the first paragraph, a disobedient child
may get many warnings, but, eventually, you are
going to say enough is enough. Like YHWH did
with Israel, you will finally get that divorce. Like
some parents are forced to, you may have to remove
your rebellious child from your home. There is a
line in the sand. Don't cross it. Repent and come
back to the ways of the Father.

DEMS DA RULES

"God's word contained in the Bible has furnished all necessary rules to direct our conduct"-Noah Webster, author of the Webster's dictionary.

Deuteronomy 5:19 *Oh that they had such a heart as this always, to fear me and to keep all my commandments, that it might go well with them and with their descendants forever!*

By now I hope I have convinced you that laws still apply and are to be followed because that is YHWH's love language. Not to be followed for salvation, but because we love and desire a closer walk with the Father. In this chapter, we will go over general commandments that apply to everyone. As you search out the truth of the Torah more, you will find some commandments apply only to men, some only to women, and some only to children. There are some that only apply to farmers and some that only apply to Levites. There are some laws that although they are still true and commanded can't be observed, because our governments are not Torah law-based governments. And we are not in YHWH's holy land. Some laws can't be observed because the physical temple in Jerusalem is no more. It is said that there are six hundred and thirteen laws. Although I have never sat down and counted, I feel that there are not. All these laws still hold as statutes forever. But until Yeshua comes back and the governing law of the world is the Torah, we can't fully exercise our ability to do them.

Joshua 1:8 This Book of the Law shall not depart from your mouth, but you shall meditate on it day and night, so that you may be careful to do according to all that is written in it. For then you will make your way prosperous, and then you will have good success.

Joshua 22:5 Only be very careful to observe the commandment and the law that Moses the servant of the LORD commanded you, to love the LORD

your God, and to walk in all his ways and to keep
his commandments and to cling to him and to serve
him with all your heart and with all your soul."

Let's first examine the laws that can be followed
completely and fully with no exception.

Exodus 20:3 *You shall have no other gods*
before Me

Sounds pretty simple, no Ba'al, Zeus, Apollo
etc. Don't worship them. Consider though what it
means to worship.

Strongs definition of worship, shâchâh, shaw-
khaw'; a primitive root; to depress, i.e. prostrate
(especially reflexive, in homage to royalty or God):
—bow (self) down, crouch, fall down (flat), humbly
beseech, do (make) obeisance, do reverence, make
to stoop, worship. (*Strong's H7812*)

What else could this apply to? Do you have a
sports hero or team that you would fall over
yourself if you met them? Is there a movie star you
obsess about in such a way that you know
everything about them? There are people in the
world that bow down to "kings and queens" because

of the circumstances they were born or married into.
Is there someone, a minister or preacher perhaps,
that you hold their view and opinion higher than
others? I am not trying to raise up anyone's dander.
However, there is a certain minister that has written
many books and does public speaking events.
People fall over themselves to hear him speak. To
get a good seat you can pay over five thousand
dollars a ticket. He packs stadiums. Is that not
showing reverence to this man? And for what? To
hear him tell you what the Bible already does? To
hear the truth of the word? No, actually he tells you
what you want to hear (ear tickling). And people
shell out big bucks so *he* can live *his* best life.
Maybe we should really sit down and be honest
with ourselves about possible gods we put before
YHWH.

*Exodus 20:4-6 Thou shalt not make unto thee
any graven image, or any likeness of any thing that
is in heaven above, or that is in the earth beneath,
or that is in the water under the earth Thou shalt
not bow down thyself to them, nor serve them: for I
the LORD thy God am a jealous God, visiting the
iniquity of the fathers upon the children unto the*

third and fourth generation of them that hate me;
And shewing mercy unto thousands of them that
love me, and keep my commandments.

This is a pretty clear cut one, and I believe it
goes hand in hand with number one. But much like
the Pharisees of the day, people now want to put up
fences and add to the word. Does this mean that cat
statue by the fireplace or that frog in your garden
has to be tossed in the trash? No, because you are
not and have no intention of praying to the frog.
You don't in any form bow to it. You aren't going
to serve it. However, if you feel convicted about it,
then toss it. I would like to point out that there are
some who have Christ on a cross on their walls or in
their churches, and they *pray to it*. This to me, is no
different than those in Exodus who made a golden
calf in honor of YHWH and worshiped it (didn't
fare well for them.) One could even argue that if
you have a cross or picture of Yeshua, or any
religious symbol you bow down and pray in front of
daily, and feel incomplete or shamed if you don't, is
an idol. There are some people who worship these
statues that, for whatever reason cry or weep oil or
blood. No matter how miraculous it seems, it still

83

should not be worshiped. Just consider, do you have idols in your life you need to remove?

Exodus 20:7 *Thou shalt not take the name of the LORD thy God in vain; for the LORD will not hold him guiltless that taketh his name in vain.*

Many people that teach and believe that this means do not say the G-D word. While this may be crass and distasteful, it doesn't really apply for two reasons. God is not truly his name, and YHWH damns things all the time. When someone says it, they are essentially asking for YHWH to bring damnation onto something. So, let's take a look at what the words, "in vain" mean.

Strongs Definition of vain shâv^e', shawv; or shav; from the same as H7722 in the sense of desolating; evil (as destructive), literally (ruin) or morally (especially guile); figuratively idolatry (as false, subjective), uselessness (as deceptive, objective; also adverbially, in vain):—false(-ly), lie, lying, vanity (*Strong's H7722*)

Consider the word, "vain" and its definitions. Does it not make more sense that taking YHWH's name in vain is making a sworn oath in his name? "I swear to God/YHWH," and have no intention of actually doing it, or not completing your oath because of laziness or how it makes you look in the eyes of others? It could also mean destroying something or someone because it personally offends you, and saying it is because YHWH told you to or in honor of Him, lying about something and saying YHWH told you to do to it, only to justify your own evil intent and actions—like blowing up an abortion clinic, for example. Although abortion is evil, YHWH did not tell someone to kill and endanger people by blowing it up.

There is another way to look at this. We were made in YHWH's image. However, we all look, sound, and think differently. Could this mean more than just appearance? I believe this means we are to emulate YHWH just like Yeshua did. We were created in His name. When you don't follow His instructions or you act in a way that Yeshua would not, you are taking the name of YHWH in vain.

2 Corinthians 3:18 *And we all, with unveiled face, beholding the glory of the Lord, are being transformed into the same image from one degree of* *glory to another. For this comes from the Lord who is the Spirit.*

Exodus 20:8-11 *Remember my Sabbath and keep it holy. Six days shalt thou labour, and do all thy work: But the seventh day is the sabbath of the LORD thy God: in it thou shalt not do any work, thou, nor thy son, nor thy daughter, thy manservant, nor thy maidservant, nor thy cattle, nor thy stranger that is within thy gates: For in six days the LORD made heaven and earth, the sea, and all that in them is, and rested the seventh day: wherefore the LORD blessed the sabbath day, and hallowed it.*

There are a few things to consider with this. This is the only commandment of the BIG TEN we are commanded to remember. This could be for a myriad of reasons. YHWH knew the Catholic church would change the day from Friday evening to Saturday evening to a Sunday to avoid looking "too Jewish". It could also be that He knew we would eventually become so busy in our lives that setting aside a day for fellowship with Him and not working, buying, or selling for twenty-four hours could become almost impossible. I also think it's so we would remember His holy days, which are themselves or contain in them a Sabbath day (We will go into more detail on the commanded feasts later.).

Exodus 20:12 *Honour thy father and thy mother: that thy days may be long upon the land which the LORD thy God giveth thee.*

Full Disclosure, before I came to the truth and understanding of Torah, I had a lot of trouble with this. What did honor mean? Was it respect? Was it doing whatever they told or ask of me? If my parents did something illegal, and I reported it to the police, would I be breaking this commandment? How many times did I talk to someone about something I viewed as wrong that my parents did and heard, "Hey they are still your parent," as if that was the exception to every rule and a reason to look the other way? My parents are divorced, if one gave me an order in direct opposition to what the other said, who was I to honor? So admittedly this was one of those I glossed over mostly due to my lack of understanding. In the Bible, what gave a parent heartache and dishonor was when their child went away from YHWH and did not follow His laws. In some cases, to such a degree that if an adult child would not repent, they were brought before the city judges and could be stoned. *119ministries* has a great video, *Should We Stone Our Children*, that explains this brilliantly. To honor your mother and father is to follow the Torah and be pleasing to YHWH.

Exodus 20:13 *"Thou Shalt Not Murder"* is pretty clear cut. Yet, there are some things to consider here as well. A favorite argument a lot of non-believers like to say is, "There are too many contradictions in the Bible." The will say such things as, "You're not to murder, but you can stone someone to death if they are gay?!" or, "Tell that to the people of Jericho!" I have even heard believers say that due to this commandment they would not defend themselves or their family if someone was going to try to kill them. Since taking the would-be murderer's life, they would be breaking this commandment. So, what would be considered murder in the Bible? The Bible's usage of this word is very clear; *to murder, slay, kill* (Qal) to murder, slay, premeditated... *(Strongs H7031)*

Jeremiah 22:3 Thus saith the LORD; Execute ye judgment and righteousness, and deliver the spoiled out of the hand of the oppressor: and do no wrong, do no violence to the stranger, the fatherless, nor the widow, neither shed innocent blood in this place.

Do not set out with the intention of killing anyone. Accidentally killing someone is not under this command. In the Torah, there is actually a law requiring sanctuary cities for people who accidently kill someone. You are allowed to defend yourself, family, and your possessions from anyone who seeks to bring them or you harm. If killing with malice of forethought is against the Bible and YHWH doesn't break his own laws, how are the wars and battles in the old testament directed by Him not breaking the law? It wasn't murder as defined here. YHWH allows you to kill to stop the spread of evil through bloodlines. The cities that Israel attacked were evil. The entire city must be uprooted, children and all because of it. One of the more popular arguments that I agree with states these cities were not wholly human. They were descended from tainted blood of the Nephilim For more detailed teachings on this, please look at Rob Skiba's *Babylon Rising* and *Archon Invasion* videos and books. If you believe, as I do, that these populations were not fully human beings, they were descendants of the fallen angels, then the rule wouldn't apply anyway. They are not able to receive redemption. They have no souls to save. Killing the entire population held a logistical tactic as well. If someone killed my father and my entire city populace, when I got to fighting age, I would try to avenge my father and my city. You see, this happens a lot with wars. Children grow up in the wreckage as orphans and become embittered and seek vengeance. If there is no one left, there is no revenge. The war ends in one generation.

Exodus 20:14 *Thou shalt not commit adultery.*

Strictly speaking, the Strong's definition of this law is directed towards women. However, this does not give a man carte blanche to go out cheating. The Bible says that you are to love your wife as Christ loves the church. Yeshua and YHWH are forever faithful to us. You also take an oath before YHWH to forsake all others. Yeshua said to look at a woman in lust is to commit adultery in your heart. So, if you cheat on your wife, you're not only a jerk, you're taking YHWH's name in vain. "Yes, but what about the adulterous woman in the New Testament? Jesus forgave her. Don't judge!" This is why knowing the Torah is so important. When a city is run by Torah law, the adulterers, the man and the woman, had to be brought before the judges at the city gates with two or three witnesses. Hence, when Yeshua said, "*let no man without sin cast the first stone,*" He was pointing this out. The man wasn't with her, they weren't at the city gates, they had no witnesses. Yeshua, although the Messiah, was not viewed as a judge by those in the city. Had anyone thrown the stone or had Yeshua, they and He would have been in violation of the Torah and sinned.

Exodus 20:15 *Thou shalt not steal.*

This one is self-explanatory. Don't take things that do not belong to you. Spoils of war obviously are not included in this. You may say, "Well, what if you are really hungry and can't afford food?" Well, in the Torah, farmers were to leave the last of their crops for the poor and orphans. Today there are food banks and shelters that offer this service. However, there have been times in the Bible when the Torah was broken to save a life. For example,

91

the midwives who lied to Pharaoh about Hebrew children being born before they arrived so they wouldn't have to kill them as ordered, or when David stole the show bread to save himself from starving. So, if it comes down to you or your family literally starving to death, then I am pretty sure you won't be in grievous violation of the Torah.

Exodus 20:16 *Thou shalt not bear false witness against thy neighbor.*

Do not lie about your neighbor, as we discussed when talking about adultery. Being a witness to someone's transgressions can lead to serious and deadly consequences to the transgressor. This one holds many possible punishments for you. Lying about another person breaking a commandment whose punishment is death, you are now a murderer. You are now taking YHWH's name in vain. You are now stealing this man's/woman's life, as well as the time and financial security that they bring to their families. So instead of breaking one commandment, you are breaking four. With some of those commandments, the punishment is death.

Exodus 20:17 *Thou shalt not covet thy*

*neighbor's house, thou shalt not covet thy
neighbor's wife, nor his manservant, nor his
maidservant, nor his ox, nor his ass, nor anything
that is thy neighbor's.*

Don't be envious of what someone else has or
gets. You can admire something and not envy it to
the point it breeds anger and contempt. However,
sometimes envy does happen. An extreme example
is Cain and Abel. Cain was envious of Abel getting
the blessing from YHWH and killed him. Envy
leads to hate. Hate can lead to murder, theft,
adultery, lying, and one could even argue that you
can become so envious it becomes an idol or a false
god to you.

Those are the main ten everyone says they
follow. Hopefully, I have shown how some of the
other commandments mentioned and not cited help
explain the Big Ten.

Now let's take a look at some others that are
easily followed without an exception.

Leviticus 17:10 *"If any one of the House of
Israel or of the strangers who sojourn among them*

eats any blood, I will set my face against that person who eats blood and will cut him off from among his people. For the life of the flesh is in the blood, and I have given it for you on the altar to make atonement for your souls, for it is the blood that makes atonement by the life.

No vampirism or literal Bloody Mary's! Now, most people go all crazy on this one, and seem to think that you can't eat your steaks rare or enjoy beef tartar. That is not what this is talking about. This is talking about the blood that holds life. Hemoglobin carries oxygen (the breath of life) throughout the body. Myoglobin is specific to the muscle. When an animal is butchered, the hemoglobin-rich blood is drained. So, when you are eating red meat, the muscle, it is myoglobin. If you feel convicted to burn your steak to shoe leather consistency, go ahead.

Unfortunately, there are people out there who will sacrifice an animal or a human still today to false gods or Satan, pour the blood in a cup and drink it. This is a flat-out sin. Do not do it. I would avoid movies and books that glorify these acts as well. There are also some people who believe that you can't have a life-saving blood transfusion from another person. I would say to pray on this. I personally do not feel this applies to the commandment, and if it does, again you can break Torah law to save a life.

Leviticus 7:23-25 *"Speak to the people of Israel, saying, You shall eat no fat, of ox or sheep or goat. The fat of an animal that dies of itself and the fat of one that is torn by beasts may be put to any other use, but on no account shall you eat For every person who eats of the fat of an animal of which a food offering may be made to the LORD shall be cut off from his people.*

This can be very confusing because most meats are marbled with fat. Well, fear not. The scriptures yet again define themselves! The fat mentioned is actually specified in other verses.

Exodus 29:22 *"You shall also take the fat from the ram and the fat tail and the fat that covers the entrails, and the long lobe of the liver and the two kidneys with the fat that is on them, and the right thigh (for it is a ram of ordination),"*

95

Leviticus 3:4 *and the two kidneys with the fat that is on them at the loins, and the long lobe of the liver that he shall remove with the kidneys.*

The fat that surrounds the inner organs, the kidneys, and the rump are not to be eaten. If the animal was not sacrificed and the fat burned at the altar, then they were used for other things like candle making and greasing wagon wheels. Nothing was wasted. Your well-marbled pot roast is safe to be eaten!

Leviticus 18:6 *"None of you shall approach any one of his close relatives to uncover nakedness. I am the LORD."*

Leviticus 7-18 goes into the more specific descriptions of close relatives, but it all comes down to this. Do not sleep with your family members, this means no siblings, daughters, sons, mothers or mothers-in-law, no step-mothers or children, no aunts or uncles. For most people, this is a no brainer. But we have all seen a Jerry Springer episode to know that it's not clear cut for everyone. The more this world "progresses," the more depravity we are seeing accepted as the norm.

Leviticus 18:19 *"You shall not approach a woman to uncover her nakedness while she is in her menstrual uncleanness.*

Do not have sex with your wife while she is on her period.

Leviticus 18:20 *And you shall not lie sexually with your neighbor's wife and so make yourself unclean with her.*

These are covered in the Big Ten. Do not have sex with anyone's wife, except your own. We are all each other's neighbors.

Leviticus 18:21 *You shall not give any of your children to offer them to Molech, and so profane the name of your God: I am the LORD.*

I know as you read this you are thinking, who nowadays sacrifices to Molech?! But think about this. Are there no organizations that kill babies regularly? Molech is just another name for Satan. As I write this book, the city of New York has made it legal to kill children up to the minute before they are born. Is that not a sacrifice to evil?

Psalm 139:13 *For you formed my inward parts; you knitted me together in my mother's womb.*

YHWH knows everyone before they draw breath, creating them individually. Aborting them is an affront to him.

Leviticus 18:22 *You shall not lie with a male as with a woman; it is an abomination.*

Homosexuality is a sin, an abomination. YHWH made us to go forth and multiply. This cannot happen with two males or two females having sex. There is now a call for the LGBT community to be allowed to openly practice their sins while being a part of the church clergy. This is a sin. An entire city was destroyed with a flood partly because of it, and people want to welcome it into the church. People like to argue that you are born homosexual, that it is genetic. If that were the case, every set of identical twins would have the same sexual orientation. They do not. If people were born that way, it would not be against the word of YHWH.

Leviticus 18:23 *And you shall not lie with any*

animal and so make yourself unclean with it,
neither shall any woman give herself to an animal
to lie with it: it is perversion.

Recently in Canada, there was a legal
determination stating it is not illegal to have sex
with animals. This is horrific, not only because it is
a sin, but it tortures the animal. Usually, this is
causing its death, or the need for it to be put down
due to internal damage. There are some religions
who have sex with goats and think it is ok. This is
the same religion that believes it's ok to marry
toddlers.

Exodus 23:19 *The first of the first fruits of your*
ground you shall bring into the house of Yahweh
your God. "You shall not boil a young goat in its
mother's milk.

This does not mean you cannot eat
cheeseburgers. It doesn't mean you can't have meat
and cheese together. Abraham served meat and
cheese to YHWH and the angels who visited him.
This could mean a few different things. No one
specifically knows why. There are speculations of it
pertaining to Pagan witchcraft or worship. But if

you have a goat, do not boil it in its mother's milk.

Deut. 14:21 *You shall not eat of anything that dies of itself: you may give it to the foreigner living among you who is within your gates, that he may eat it; or you may sell it to a foreigner: for you are a holy people to Yahweh your God. You shall not boil a young goat in its mother's milk.*

Again, don't boil that goat in its mother's milk. Don't eat animals that have died on their own. I know it seems kinder to wait until one of your animals lives a very long life, but YHWH commands that we do not eat them that way.

Numbers 15:38 "Speak to the people of Israel, and tell them to make tassels on the corners of their garments throughout their generations, and to put a cord of blue on the tassel of each corner. And it shall be a tassel for you to look at and remember all the commandments of the LORD, to do them, not to follow after your own heart and your own eyes, which you are inclined to whore after. So you shall remember and do all my commandments, and be holy to your God.

Deuteronomy 22:12 *"You shall make yourself tassels on the four corners of the garment with which you cover yourself.*

Remember in the 1990s and early 2000s church members would wear bracelets saying WWJD? It was a brilliant idea reminding people to walk as Christ walked. But had people dug into the scripture, they would have seen that it was unnecessary. YHWH had it covered in the form of tzitzits. These little tassels are to remind you of the commandments and to always walk in the ways of the Father. Most people wear four of them on their belt loops. I usually don't have belt loops, so I wear a crocheted belt that I connect them to. Some people believe they are only for men, but it does not specify gender. It is also a commonly held belief that when the woman who suffered from the bleeding touched the hem of Yeshua's garment, she was actually touching his tzitzits.

Numbers 30:2 *If a man vows a vow to the LORD, or swears an oath to bind himself by a pledge, he shall not break his word. He shall do according to all that proceeds out of his mouth.*

101

A man is only as good as his word. Most people today make empty promises and break the commandment of taking YHWH's name in vain. It's a part of the Big Ten. Do not swear to do something you have no intention of doing.

Deuteronomy 15:7-8 *"If among you, one of your brothers should become poor, in any of your towns within your land that the LORD your God is giving you, you shall not harden your heart or shut your hand against your poor brother, but you shall open your hand to him and lend him sufficient for his need, whatever it may be.*

I learned a long time ago, never loan money that you intend to get back. If you are able to help those in poverty, those in need, do so. If you have to choose between that new shiny game console or giving that money to a homeless mother who doesn't have food for her kids, give to the mother. Or if you have a cousin who has lost his job and just needs a little bump to keep his head above water, I would hope that you would give and give generously.

Deuteronomy 19:15 *"A single witness shall not*

suffice against a person for any crime or for any wrong in connection with any offense that he has committed. Only on the evidence of two witnesses or of three witnesses shall a charge be established."

Although this law actually applies to Torah based judicial systems, it's a good one to put into practice. This prevents people from a "he said she said" issue that plagues many relationships and court cases today. I am not saying that crimes should not be reported. They absolutely should. But a case with more than one witness is a stronger case. In the cases of rape, DNA and other physical evidence serve as a second witness to the crime.

Deuteronomy 22:1-3 *"You shall not see your brother's ox or his sheep going astray and ignore them. You shall take them back to your brother And if he does not live near you and you do not know who he is, you shall bring it home to your house, and it shall stay with you until your brother seeks it. Then you shall restore it to him. And you shall do the same with his donkey or with his garment, or with any lost thing of your brother's, which he loses and you find; you may not ignore it.*

If you find something that is lost, find the owner. While you are looking for that owner, take care of it. You are responsible for it until that owner is found, even if, in your opinion, a responsible person shouldn't have lost it to begin with. You are to return it to them whole and intact.

Deuteronomy 22:4 *You shall not see your brother's donkey or his ox fallen down by the way and ignore them. You shall help him to lift them up again.*

I liken this one to seeing someone with a flat tire or car trouble at the side of the road. If you are able to help them, pull over and help, or call an emergency company to help them. ALWAYS use caution, and do not put yourself in danger. Obviously, not everyone has pure intentions in those situations.

Deuteronomy 22:5 *"A woman shall not wear a man's garment, nor shall a man put on a woman's cloak, for whoever does these things is an abomination to the LORD your God."*

Some folks think this means women should only

wear dresses. However, jeans and pants are designed specifically for a male or a female. This verse is for men and women who dress in the clothes of the opposite sex, because they want to look like them. This is referring to cross-dressers, drag kings and queens, and the transgenders of the world. Not for a woman who wears jeans or her husband's t-shirt, or a man who wears a sleep gown to bed (sleep gown—not a nighty intended for a female).

Deuteronomy 22:8 *"When you build a new house, you shall make a parapet for your roof, that you may not bring the guilt of blood upon your house, if anyone should fall from it.*

Safety First! Put a railing up on balconies and ledges of your roof so that no one will fall off by accident.

Deuteronomy 23:19 *"You shall not charge interest on loans to your brother, interest on money, interest on food, interest on anything that is lent for interest.*

Don't try to profit from kindness. If you loan a

105

fellow believer money, and they swear an oath to pay you back, do not charge a fee to them for the use of the money.

Deuteronomy 23:20 *You may charge a foreigner interest, but you may not charge your brother interest, that the LORD your God may bless you in all that you undertake in the land that you are entering to take possession of it.*

You can choose to charge unbelievers interest on loans. However, kindness is its own reward.

Deuteronomy 23:21 *"If you make a vow to the LORD your God, you shall not delay fulfilling it, for the LORD your God will surely require it of you, and you will be guilty of sin.*

I think most of us are guilty of breaking this one. "If you grant this to me, YHWH, I will donate my first $1000 to such and such charity." And then we "forget". We should probably not do that.

Deuteronomy 23:22-23 *But if you refrain from vowing, you will not be guilty of sin. You shall be careful to do what has passed your lips, for you have voluntarily vowed to the LORD your God what* *you have promised with your mouth.*

Don't make promises you can't or won't keep.

Deuteronomy 25:13-15 *"You shall not have in your bag two kinds of weights, a large and a small. You shall not have in your house two kinds of measures, a large and a small. A full and fair weight you shall have, a full and fair measure you shall have, that your days may be long in the land that the LORD your God is giving you.*

Be honest in your business dealings. Don't overcharge. Be honest about its worth.

Leviticus 19:19 *Ye shall keep my statutes. Thou shalt not let thy cattle gender with a diverse kind: thou shalt not sow thy field with mingled seed: neither shall a garment mingled of linen and woolen come upon thee.*

If I had a nickel for every time someone has said to me, "Unless you're wearing 100% cotton clothes, you are breaking the law," Or "Well, if the law still applies, you're going to hell for wearing a cotton/poly blend," I could probably pay off my student loans. And admittedly, before reading all

107

five books of Torah, I was feverishly searching the internet for cheap, all cotton clothes. But that was before understanding that the law was explained more in Deuteronomy.

Deuteronomy 22:11 *You shall not wear cloth of wool and linen mixed together.*

It speaks specifically of wool and linen here, not other mixes. Why? Well, there are things called frequency studies. These studies actually test the frequency of objects (apparently everything has one). Since YHWH spoke the world into motion, this makes sense. Wool and linen have the same frequency. These studies also show that wearing fabrics of the same frequency will make a person ill.

YHWH does not like things mixing. He doesn't like hybrids. I am not talking about two humans of different color marrying and having a child. That's racist ignorance. I am talking about the blending of different KINDS, like a rat and a pig, or a human with any animal. I urge you to look into the Nephilim. Rob Skiba has many great videos on this topic. YHWH also doesn't like mixing Pagan practices and beliefs with the worship of Him.

Leviticus 19:27 *Ye shall not round the corners of your heads, neither shalt thou mar the corners of thy beard.*

This does not mean that you cannot shave. In ancient times some Pagan practices of mourning included shaving your head or violently plucking out the corners of your beard. Some religious practices still today have people shave their head when they mourn the dead. Some races cannot grow beards, or they are patchy. Are they damned because they can't grow a beard?

Leviticus 19:28 *Ye shall not make any cuttings in your flesh for the dead, nor print any marks upon you: I am the LORD.*

I have my ears pierced, and I have tattoos. I got them before I started my walk with Torah. However, I am not opposed to them. This commandment brings a lot of arguments among the community, particularly because of the marks. Some scripture translations say tattoos. The practice of blood-letting for mourning is from Pagan rituals. A great example of this is in the movie, *Dances With Wolves*. The main female character was

109

mourning her husband by slicing her skin and bleeding. This is what the cutting of flesh means. It is not referring to piercing your ears. Most people tend to skip over the "in remembrance of the dead" portion. The markings part is what brings arguments. A very educated Torah teacher, who happens to hate tattoos, once said that there is no mention of markings in the original Greek and Hebrew writings. These were added later on. However, even if this is accurate and we aren't to mark ourselves, I would still like to point out this still applied to "in remembrance of the dead". If you feel this refers to all tattoos and piercings, I would say pray about it and go with your convictions. But do not look down on or judge those who don't view this the same way. After all, Isaac marked Rebecca as his wife by piercing her nose.

Numbers 10:10 *Also in the day of your gladness, and in your solemn days, and in the beginnings of your months, ye shall blow with the trumpets over your burnt offerings, and over the sacrifices of your peace offerings; that they may be to you for a memorial before your God: I am the LORD your God.*

Every New Moon we are to blow our Shofars (horns from rams). My husband tries to blow the Shofar, but it can be difficult. I have heard that it is because we bought a short one. I usually find a YouTube video of someone blowing the Shofar and play that as well. No, we do not have burnt offerings. But we do blow the Shofar on the new moon.

Most people follow these laws without even thinking about it. There are some that people choose to ignore much to their own detriment. Dive into the word. Research and look into the laws. Apply and observe all you can. The ultimate sacrifice of Yeshua covers our sin by HIS blood. We still must obey the laws as best we can and know in the millennial reign, all of them will be understood, and we will be able to observe all without exception.

FOOD FIGHT!

Lev 11:2-3 *"Speak to the people of Israel,*
saying, These are the living things that you may eat
among all the animals that are on the eat. Whatever
parts the hoof and is cloven-footed and chews the
cud, among the animals, you may eat..."

This by far has got to be my favorite part of the
Torah to talk about. I am a foodie. I love food and
discovering new ways to recreate old classics. So,
when I discovered that a lot of the "foods" I loved
were not allowed, I was so upset. I tried to reason it
away. I told myself what I had always been told
made sense—that they were forbidden because the
Hebrews lacked the culinary knowledge to cook the
foods to a safe temperature. But then I thought
about it. If YHWH was speaking directly to Moses,
as it says in the Bible, why didn't he just tell him to
cook it to a certain degree and not forbid it? My

excuse no longer held water. So, I exchanged my pork bacon for turkey and turned away from Lobster-fest. However, I still wanted to know why.

As it turns out, there are so many reasons not to consider those animals food, it's surprising the FDA allows them to be sold. Let's go for the one that hurts everyone the most, bacon, or more specifically pork. I once read a study that 90% of former meat eaters that became vegetarians stated the one thing they missed from their former lifestyle was bacon. Before digging into this topic, I really sympathized.

Leviticus 11:7 And the pig, because it parts the hoof and is cloven-footed but does not chew the cud, is unclean to you. You shall not eat any of their flesh, and you shall not touch their carcasses; they are unclean to you.

Just a little warning, this topic may be stomach-turning if you are currently eating.

If you have spent any time on a farm with pigs, you quickly realize that these are not nature's cleanest creatures. They wallow in anything and everything. Mud, poop, blood, decaying foods, you name it they will wallow in it, and they will eat it. Pigs will eat their own poop and pee, your poop, the dog's poop. They have also been shown to eat cancerous tumors and their own testicles if gelded. And unfortunately, they will kill and eat their own young. Pigs digest food in about four hours. That is not enough time for their body to remove all the toxic impurities they ingest. Where do the undigested impurities and toxins go? — into that delicious fat and skin (yum!). The reason it stores in the fat is because pigs do not have sweat glands. So, the nasties can't exit the body that way either.

"According to an investigation by *Consumer Reports,* 69% of all raw pork samples tested (of about 200 samples) were contaminated with a dangerous bacteria known as Yersinia enterocolitica. These bacteria can cause fever, gastrointestinal illness, diarrhea, vomiting, and cramps.

Ground pork was more likely to be contaminated than pork chops, and also tested positive for other contaminants, including a controversial drug called ractopamine, which is banned in China and Europe. Many of the bacteria

115

found in the pork were actually resistant to multiple antibiotics. Which means, if you were to get sick, treatment would be difficult.

According to the report, "We found salmonella, staphylococcus aureus, or listeria monocytogenes, more common causes of foodborne illness, in 3 to 7 percent of samples. And 11 percent harbored enterococcus, which can indicate fecal contamination and can cause problems such as urinary-tract infections."

Pigs are host to a number of parasites, viruses, and other organisms, many of which can be directly transmitted to humans. Some include:

- **Taenia solium** — an intestinal parasite that can cause tissue infection and loss of appetite.

- **Menangle virus** — a virus that can cause fever, chills, rashes, headaches, and sweating.

- **Trichinella** — a parasitic roundworm that can cause edema, myalgia, fever, and malaise.

- **Hepatitis E** – A viral inflammation that can cause fatigue, nausea, and jaundice. More severe cases can lead to liver fibrosis and cirrhosis.

The study does indicate that if you cook pork properly, you can reduce the risk of these parasites affecting you. But there is no guaranteed temperature for safety when it comes to pork." Alanna Ketler, "Why You Should Consider Not Eating Pork", Collective Evolution, November 23, 2014, https://www.collective-evolution.com/2014/11/23/why-you-should-never-eat-pork.

A possible reduction in these nasties is not worth the risk of a possible infection of these viruses. I have not intentionally eaten pork for two years. I have found that any time I have accidentally consumed pork, I have spent hours in the bathroom realizing that pork was in the food I ate. Thank you, Jack in The Box egg rolls! It's just better to err on the side of caution.

Bring on the butter! Let's talk lobster (well, shellfish in general). First, I have to say I became less fond of lobster when I heard a scientist on *Discovery Channel* say that lobsters were the spiders of the sea. However, I would still gobble up tails whenever I could. USELESS FACT ALERT! When America was first founded, lobsters were considered peasant food and not fit for high society. They were given away to the poor, and now people spend upwards of twenty dollars or more for the tails alone!

Leviticus 11:9, 12 *These you may eat of all that are in the water: whatever in the water has fins and scales, whether in the seas or in the rivers—that you may eat…. Whatever in the water does not have fins or scales—that shall be an abomination to you.*

All Shellfish are bottom and filter feeders. They eat decaying fish and debris at the bottom of the ocean, including dead fish, poop, toxic waste, bacteria, and any other nastiness they can get their pinchers on. This means they can contain mercury and other pollutants found in the ocean.

"Foodborne illnesses are a concern when eating shellfish and other types of seafood. A number of foodborne illnesses associated with shellfish, such as Norwalk virus, Salmonella, E. coli and hepatitis A virus, come from the contamination of water by sewage. Although foodborne illness can affect anyone who comes into contact with the contaminated food, people with certain medical conditions, such as liver disease, diabetes, altered iron metabolism, gastrointestinal issues or a suppressed immune system are at higher risk." Arielle Kamps, "What Is the Risk of Shellfish?", Updated November 21, 2018, https://healthyeating.sfgate.com/risk-shellfish-2026.html.

"According to the FDA, raw oysters, mussels and clams are responsible for 85 percent of all illnesses caused by eating seafood. Such conditions as hepatitis A, salmonella, Norwalk virus, cholera, and paralytic shellfish poisoning are just a few of the problems that are often linked to shellfish consumption. The more waste we dump into our oceans, lakes, and streams, the greater the risk of getting sick from eating shellfish and other aquatic scavengers becomes." Susan Patterson, "God's Dietary Laws: Why Pigs, Crabs and Lobsters Are Bad for You", off-grid-foods, (blog), Off the Grid

News, https://www.offthegridnews.com/off-grid-
foods/gods-dietary-laws-why-pigs-crabs-and-
lobsters-are-bad-for-you/.

*Leviticus 11:10 But anything in the seas or the
rivers that does not have fins and scales, of the
swarming creatures in the waters and of the living
creatures that are in the waters, is detestable to
you. You shall regard them as detestable; you shall
not eat any of their flesh, and you shall detest their
carcasses. Everything in the waters that does not
have fins and scales is detestable to you.*

YHWH said these things are detestable to you.
He wanted to get the point across so much He said
it three times! Goodbye, calamari. Later, lobster.
See-ya, shrimp and scallops. There are plenty of
fish in the sea. Just make sure they have scales and
fins.

Bye-Bye birdie! If you read Leviticus 11:13-19,
it goes over the various birds that are not on the
menu. So, the next time you go to the exotic meats
section at Trader Joes, remember that ostrich is off
limits. The birds listed are scavengers (are you
noticing the theme yet?) or predators. They feed off

the carcasses and blood of other animals. This leads to the transmission of disease and environmental toxins. There are a few debates you will find among the biblically clean eaters about chickens or emu being unclean. Zach Baur from *New2Torah* did a simple, short video explaining why these birds are clean and ready for the BBQ.

Leviticus 11:20 *"All winged insects that go on all fours are detestable to you.*

Leviticus 11:21-23 *Yet among the winged insects that go on all fours you may eat those that have jointed legs above their feet, with which to hop on the ground. Of them you may eat: the locust of any kind, the bald locust of any kind, the cricket of any kind, and the grasshopper of any kind. But all other winged insects that have four feet are detestable to you.*

Chocolate-covered crickets anyone? Although I, myself have yet to eat bugs (aside from the occasional gnat that has flown in my mouth without permission), many cultures in the Middle East and Asia have crickets and locusts as a mainstay in their diets, for good reason. Locusts are an excellent source of protein and contain a variety of fatty acids and minerals. But other bugs are off limits. That means all the tequila worms you ate on a dare in college, were not clean.

Now, this is where most people would bring up a few well meaning, but heavily misinterpreted scripture passages to prove that all food is clean. Before we dive into that little gem, let me state this, "Yes, all food is clean." Those animals I mentioned are not food. So that means, we, having dominion over all animals or saying thanksgiving over them, will not make them food and will not make them clean. Let's get into the top two arguments.

Peter's Vision

Acts 10:9-16 *The next day, as they were on their journey and approaching the city, Peter went up on the housetop about the sixth hour to pray. And he became hungry and wanted something to eat, but while they were preparing it, he fell into a trance and saw the heavens opened and something like a great sheet descending, being let down by its four corners upon the earth. In it were all kinds of animals and reptiles and birds of the air. And there*

came a voice to him: "Rise, Peter; kill and eat."
But Peter said, "By no means, Lord; for I have
never eaten anything that is common or unclean."
And the voice came to him again a second time,
"What God has made clean, do not call common.
"This happened three times, and the thing was
taken up at once to heaven.

Now anyone who reads these passages, of
course, will read it and think, Bring on the bacon!
However, if you only read a few more passages,
you will come to the conclusion that it doesn't mean
eat whatever you want.

Acts 10:17 *Now while Peter was inwardly*
perplexed as to what the vision that he had seen
might mean, behold, the men who were sent by
Cornelius, having made inquiry for Simon's house,
stood at the gate and called out to ask whether
Simon who was called Peter was lodging there.

Why would Peter be mulling over what the
meaning of the vision meant if it were just as simple
as YHWH opening up the buffet options more? It
seems like a pretty straight forward vision.
Everything's up for grabs. No animal is safe from

the plate now. Maybe it's because the vision was not about unclean animals at all.

Act 10:19-21 And while Peter was pondering the vision, the Spirit said to him, "Behold, three men are looking for you, Rise and go down and accompany them without hesitation, for I have sent them. And Peter went down to the men and said, "I am the one you are looking for. What is the reason for your coming?

In Peter's vision, he was presented with the unclean foods three times, and now three men appear at his door looking for him, sent by the Holy Spirit. Coincidence? Probably not— a good rule of thumb when it comes to the scriptures, nothing is unimportant, and there are never coincidences. The next six verses describe his encounter with the Roman Centurion, a Gentile who the Jews said was unclean. Acts 10:28 is where it all comes together.

Acts 10:28-29 And he said to them, "You yourselves know how unlawful it is for a Jew to associate with or to visit anyone of another nation, but God has shown me that I should not call any person common or unclean. So when I was sent for,

I came without objection. I ask then why you sent for me."

It did not take Peter very long pondering to figure out what the vision meant. One of the many things Yeshua preached against was adding to the scriptures. Jews added to the Torah, built extra walls around it, so even the most moronic of them could not break the laws. But even though they didn't break their own rules and regulations, they didn't follow the laws of YHWH out of love in their hearts. Conclusion: Peter's vision was about calling Gentiles unclean, not about being able to eat anything you want.

Jesus said that all foods were clean?

Mark 7:18-19 *And he said to them," Then are you also without understanding? Do you not see that whatever goes into a person from outside cannot defile him, since it enters not his heart but his stomach, and is expelled?" (Thus, he declared all foods clean.)*

I want to point out that the vision and explanation by Peter happened *after* the crucifixion of Yeshua. If Yeshua declared foods clean when He was with Peter, why would Peter have said in his vision that he has never eaten anything, "that has been called unclean"? Wouldn't he have enjoyed a ham sandwich with Yeshua if it was declared food already?

Back to this scripture. This one, I have to say really, really makes me angry, not because of the misinterpretation. Again, without context, one could make that conclusion. Do you see the words in parenthesis? The publisher of the ESV decided to interject their interpretation as a proclamation right there in the scriptures. They were so gutsy with their assumption! They didn't even put it as a footnote, but slapped it right there beside the words of Yeshua like they hopped into a souped-up DeLorean and asked Him themselves!

deep breath, deep breath, deep breath

Again, let's look at the context of the actual comment. In Mark 7:1-5, it describes the indignation of the Pharisees who were watching Yeshua and the Apostles eat with unwashed hands. The Pharisees had traditions of washing hands and special prayers that are not a part of the Torah, but they had made into law.

Mark 7:5 And the Pharisees and the scribes asked him, "Why do your disciples not walk according to the tradition of the elders, but eat with defiled hands?"

In the scriptures following, Yeshua reprimanded and explained to them that their laws were not of YHWH's laws. It is the heart and what comes from it that can defile a person, not unwashed hands. The chapter in Mark had nothing to do with abolishing food laws. In fact, in context, it had nothing to do with food at all. I said it in the beginning of this chapter, all foods are clean! But all animals are not food!

Just to bring this to a little more personal level and understanding, would you eat your family dog? Probably not. In fact, the thought probably offends you. But some countries will eat Fido before Bessie the cow.

A few years ago, there was a huge uproar in the news, because, in Europe, Burger King used horse meat in their burgers. People went bonkers. All over social media, there were calls to boycott and have them shut down. Why then is pork accepted on your Rodeo Burger? Even though Pigs are disgusting, they are one of the smartest, most sentient animals on the planet. Yet no one turns down bacon.

In the 80s and early 90s, the tuna industry caused quite a stir when they were found to have Flipper's cousins in the can. Yet no one thinks twice about boiling a living lobster as it screams.

The forbidden animals in the Bible are banned for many reasons, but it all comes down to this— not all animals are food. So, don't eat the vacuum cleaners. Why? — because YHWH said so. If you believe YHWH doesn't care what you eat, maybe you should go back to Genesis and re-read why Adam and Eve got kicked out of Eden. They ate what YHWH told them not to.

The Mo-ha what now?

Isaiah 1:9-16 Except the LORD of hosts had left unto us a very small remnant, we should have been as Sodom, and we should have been like unto Gomorrah. Hear the word of the LORD, ye rulers of Sodom; give ear unto the law of our God, ye people of Gomorrah. To what purpose is the multitude of your sacrifices unto me? saith the LORD: I am full of the burnt offerings of rams, and the fat of fed beasts; and I delight not in the blood of bullocks, or of lambs, or of he goats. When ye come to appear before me, who hath required this at your hand, to tread my courts? Bring no more vain oblations; incense is an abomination unto me; the new moons and sabbaths, the calling of assemblies, I cannot away with; it is iniquity, even the solemn meeting. Your new moons and your appointed feasts my soul hateth: they are a trouble unto me; I am weary to

*bear them. And when ye spread forth your hands, I
will hide mine eyes from you: yea, when ye make
many prayers, I will not hear: your hands are full of
blood. Wash you, make you clean; put away the evil
of your doings from before mine eyes; cease to do
evil;*

Before I first started this journey, I realized my
understanding of the Bible was wrong, and I
scoured the Bible looking for understanding. Just
when I thought I was really getting it, I came across
this passage, and it was a confusing one. How could
the law still apply, how could Torah still apply if
YHWH was fed up with the feasts and appointed
times? Were they not in the Torah? Were they not
commanded? Was I completely wrong? I was a bit
heartbroken, to say the least. Then a very dear
friend pointed out to me the wording. YHWH does
not claim the appointed times and feast that He is
sick of as His. He specifically states "*YOUR holy
days.*" This was not YHWH passing the buck to
Israel. He was stating that these days were not His.
This could be for a few reasons. 1) The Israelites
had added so much to the law and holy day
observances that they were no longer recognizable

to Him. 2) They were mixing the beliefs and practices of other religions with the appointed times of YHWH. Thus, bastardizing and mutating them into days that were not His. 3) They were making up extra days, observances and practices, just like when they were brought out of Egypt. They were worshiping the golden calf as YHWH, making a new holiday. 4) They were going through the motions of the appointed times but were not observing them in their hearts. They were physically obedient because they had to be, not spiritual obedient out a desire to love and follow YHWH. But one thing you can take away from this verse is He was not referring to *His* appointed times as *He commanded them to be.* In fact, if you were to go to your favorite Bible web page and type in "your appointed times" into the search, the verse above is the only one that will pop up. And if you were to type "my appointed times" you would see what is pulled up is in reference to the appointed times YHWH has set and commanded.

In Hebrew, the appointed times are called the Moedim (Mo-ed-deam). These are the times set forth and commanded by YHWH, times to fellowship, worship and celebrate with friends and family. These days were specifically set so that we would be set apart from the rest of the world, times that we would remember when Israel was brought out of Egypt. They are also viewed by many as a foreshadowing of the timeline set forth by the Creator for major events. As I explained in the previous chapter, *But, Paul Said*, like many of the Torah laws, we can't fully observe them because we do not have a temple in Jerusalem. We won't be able to biblically and fully celebrate them until the thousand-year reign of Yeshua. Does that mean we can't observe in memorial to the best of our abilities? No! We can observe these Holy days in memorial and for practice of the times to come! And as we will see, there are some Moedim that we are commanded to observe no matter where we are at.

Sabbath

Lev 23:1-4 And the LORD spake unto Moses, saying, Speak unto the children of Israel, and say unto them, Concerning the feasts of the LORD, which ye shall proclaim to be holy convocations, even these are my feasts. Six days shall work be done: but the seventh day is the sabbath of rest, an holy convocation; ye shall do no work therein: it is the sabbath of the LORD in all your dwellings. These are the feasts of the LORD, even holy convocations, which ye shall proclaim in their seasons.

Strongs Definition of convocation miqrâ', mik-raw'; from H7121; something called out, i.e. a public meeting (the act, the persons, or the place); also, a rehearsal:—assembly, calling, convocation (*Strong's H7121*)

We have been taught that the Sabbath is Sunday. When I was little, I remember watching a movie on the *Disney Channel* called, *Johnny Tremain*. I asked my aunt why they were not allowed to work on Saturday. She said it was because they thought the Sabbath was on a Saturday, but it was on a Sunday. It wasn't until I was older that I decided to fact check this. I took a course in college called Western Religion Studies. This is where I learned that the Sabbath day was changed to Sunday by the fourth-century Catholic church. I also learned that Christmas was not Yeshua's birthday, but we will cover that in, *Are*

Holidays Holy?

Earliest historical records indicate all Torah observant people and those who followed Christ viewed the Sabbath day as Friday evening to Saturday evening. But there are those who celebrate fully on just Saturday. Some follow completely different calendars that I do not study or understand enough to speak about. But for my family, we celebrate Sabbath Friday evening to Saturday evening. The Gregorian calendar has Saturday as the seventh day of the week and Sunday is always the first. The word Saturday is noted to stem from the word Saturn or named after the god Saturn.

Further digging and research show that the word, Saturday, stems from the Germanic Samstag, which originates from the Greek and Hebrew word for Sabbath. All over the world, there are different words for the seventh day of the week, and most of them originate from the Greek and Hebrew word for Sabbath. We are commanded to remember the Sabbath and keep it holy. How is the church doing that if they won't even acknowledge that Sunday is not the true Sabbath?

Exodus 20:10-11 But the seventh day is the sabbath of the LORD thy God: in it thou shalt not do any work, thou, nor thy son, nor thy daughter, thy manservant, nor thy maidservant, nor thy cattle, nor thy stranger that is within thy gates: For in six days the LORD made heaven and earth, the sea, and all that in them is, and rested the seventh day: wherefore the LORD blessed the sabbath day, and hallowed it.

Exodus 31:14 Ye shall keep the sabbath therefore; for it is holy unto you: every one that defileth it shall surely be put to death: for whosoever doeth any work therein, that soul shall be cut off from among his people.

The command to rest and observe the Sabbath is given over twenty-two times in the Bible. It's also a commandment in the Big Ten, so it is very important, and one of the ways we can be set apart from the rest of the world.

Exodus 35:2-3 Six days shall work be done, but on the seventh day there shall be to you an holy day, a sabbath of rest to the LORD: whosoever doeth work therein shall be put to death. Ye shall kindle

135

*no fire throughout your habitations upon the
sabbath day.*

When first reading this, it makes you think that
you cannot have any kind of fire in your home. This
is one of the reasons Orthodox Jews tend not to
drive, flip light switches and even have "spark free"
elevators. Are they correct? Technically, they are
following the law. But, does this mean that during
the winter months we are to sit in the dark, freezing
to death once a week? That does not sound restful to
me. So, what are some context clues that can put
this into a little better understanding for us? The
previous scripture again stated the seventh day is for
rest and we are to do no work. Would fire not be a
major part of about every single job at that time?
You would need to boil water for cooking as well as
cleaning. You would need a fire for smelting tools,
and a host of other jobs. Even starting a fire was
work. You had to gather kindling, chop or carry
wood, and spark the fire with flint and stone. That is
not exactly as easy as a one flick Bic.

In Exodus, you will read of a man who was
stoned to death for collecting sticks on Sabbath.
Why? Was he picking them up to go play fetch with

Fido? No, he was focused on work and trying to get a jump on getting wood for work the following day. He was doing physical labor. The translation says sticks, but it doesn't specify how large those sticks were. Also, he was not observing the law in his heart; he was focused on work-related things.

Matthew 5:28 *"But I say to you that whoever looks at a woman to lust for her has already committed adultery with her in his heart."*

This same principle applies. He was not resting in his heart.

Exodus 20:10 *But the seventh day is the sabbath of the LORD thy God: in it thou shalt not do any work, thou, nor thy son, nor thy daughter, thy manservant, nor thy maidservant, nor thy cattle, nor thy stranger that is within thy gates.*

This one is easy, right? Who has servants except for the super-rich anyway? This obviously does not apply to "the every-day man" of today—right? We should think about this. How many times after church have we gone to the local Denny's or Perkins for brunch? "Welcome to Perkins, my name is

_____, and I will be your server today." A person who is working for compensation of any kind to provide you with a service is a servant. Even if it is for just one or two hours. *"Nor thy stranger within thy gates."* Even if they are not believers, you should not have them work for you. I don't want to step on any man-toes, but I could venture to say that your favorite sports team playing on Saturday is a violation of Sabbath. Watching it could be construed as them working for you. Just one woman's thoughts though.

Housewives rejoice!! You read it right ladies, no cleaning, no cooking, no folding, no housework on the Sabbath. Unfortunately, that means on Friday you work your buns off prepping two days' worth of meals. Remember, Hebrews collected double portions on Friday so they would not be collecting manna on Saturday, super cleaning on Friday so Saturday mess is not a horror show on Sunday. That isn't commanded. However, it is a very good suggestion.

Isaiah 58:13-14 *If thou turn away thy foot from the sabbath, from doing thy pleasure on my holy day; and call the sabbath a delight, the holy of the*

LORD, honourable; and shalt honour him, not doing thine own ways, nor finding thine own pleasure, nor speaking thine own words: Then shalt thou delight thyself in the LORD; and I will cause thee to ride upon the high places of the earth, and feed thee with the heritage of Jacob thy father: for the mouth of the LORD hath spoken it.

No pleasure? — seriously?! So, we can't enjoy anything? This is a very misunderstood scripture for a few reasons. If we are to have no pleasure, then we can't worship and study in the word as that is supposed to bring us pleasure. Also, Isaiah is a prophet of YHWH, so we must test everything he says with the Torah. (***Deuteronomy 13***) There is no command stating you cannot do things that are pleasing to you on Sabbath. So, what does he mean? He means work! I know it is hard to understand. In this day and age, people just work to get by and need vacations from what they do to recharge in order to face another day. But back then people learned a skill they enjoyed, usually loving it very much. It was a pleasure for them to work that job. Wouldn't that be lovely? I have loved writing this book, and even though it is Bible study 90% of the time, I still refrain from writing or researching book related scriptures on the Sabbath, because I intend to sell it. I understand there are some jobs that require work on Saturday. It's very hard to find a job that doesn't require working on at least one Saturday a month. The only thing we can do in this case is pray YHWH will deliver us to a job which allows us to wholly observe His Sabbath day. If you want to stay at your job, pray that your boss will recognize your new understanding of the Sabbath and allow you that day off. Trust and have faith that He will take care of you. Those of you who have shops open on Saturdays, close them and have faith YHWH will replace and increase the revenue you would normally receive on Saturdays to a different day, honoring your faith and obedience to His word. I know it's easier said than done. However, there are many stories about people who have been blessed observing the true Sabbath.

Now, in the next chapter, we will go over man-made traditions that are bad because they are or were practiced in the worship of false gods. Some traditions observed on the Sabbath and Holy Days are not improper if practiced. For example, there are traditions some people follow on Sabbath which come from Jewish customs that can be done, lighting candles, making challah bread, blessings over the wife and children, reading and discussing the Torah portions. Sabbath observers make a big meal and dress nice, as if they are having dinner with very important guests (YHWH and Yeshua).

Challah Bread is a sweet braided bread. They usually make two loaves to represent the double portion of manna received before Sabbath during the Exodus.

The lighting of the candles is iffy to me because when they light them, they say a prayer saying that YHWH commanded them to light the candles on Sabbath. There is no such scripture in the Torah.

The Blessing over your wife usually is said something like this, "Bless you, YHWH, King of the universe who has given me a wife and help-mate, and mother to our children."

The Blessing over the wine is usually like this, "Bless you, oh YHWH, King of the universe who has given us the fruit of the vine." Those are a few of the traditions which can be practiced, do not break the law and are fun things for your family.

Passover

Exodus 12:1-11 And the LORD spake unto Moses and Aaron in the land of Egypt, saying, This month shall be unto you the beginning of months: it shall be the first month of the year to you Speak ye unto all the congregation of Israel, saying, In the tenth day of this month they shall take to them every man a lamb, according to the house of their fathers, a lamb for an house: And if the household be too little for the lamb, let him and his neighbour next unto his house take it according to the number of the souls; every man according to his eating shall make your count for the lamb. Your lamb shall be without blemish, a male of the first year: ye shall take it out from the sheep, or from the goats: And ye shall keep it up until the fourteenth day of the same month: and the whole assembly of the congregation of Israel shall kill it in the evening. And they shall take of the blood, and strike it on the two side posts and on the upper door post of the houses, wherein they shall eat it. And they shall eat the flesh in that night, roast with fire, and unleavened bread; and with bitter herbs they shall eat it. Eat not of it raw, nor sodden at all with water, but roast with fire; his head with his legs, and with the purtenance thereof. And ye shall let nothing of it remain until the morning; and that which remaineth of it until the morning ye shall burn with fire. And thus shall ye eat it; with your loins girded, your shoes on your feet, and your staff in your hand; and ye shall eat it in haste: it is the LORD'S passover.

Passover is often confused or replaced with Easter. It is not Easter, nor does it have anything to do with it. Passover is a commanded Holy day. Although there are aspects of it we can keep, biblically speaking, it is not one we can observe in full, because we do not have a temple to sacrifice or worship at. We can observe it in memorial of what happened in Egypt and in practice of what will come during the millennial reign. It also can be a very fun and enjoyable meal event!

Exodus 12:21 *Then Moses called for all the elders of Israel, and said unto them, Draw out and take you a lamb according to your families, and kill* *the Passover.*

This is actually the main part of Passover that we can't observe without a temple. Most of us do not have access to a lamb that is no older than a year or have the knowledge to slaughter it. Thank YHWH for the butcher shop! We do not buy a whole lamb as we are a small family, and you aren't to leave any until morning. So, we get enough for one or two servings each person, like a boneless lamb leg or small rack of lamb. You do not need to have lamb at Passover supper, but most people do. If you are a vegetarian or vegan, I am sure you would be able to find a good substitute.

Exodus 12:22 *And ye shall take a bunch of hyssop, and dip it in the blood that is in the bason, and strike the lintel and the two side posts with the blood that is in the bason; and none of you shall go out at the door of his house until the morning.*

This goes hand in hand with the sacrifice of the lamb. You can't do it. Also, most of our doors do not have a blood basin at the threshold. *119ministries* has a great video on the threshold covenant. Basically, Hebrews had basins or cups built into their doorways that they would fill with the blood of a sacrificed animal for agreements or covenants. One thing I will be implementing with my family this year, something I learned from Steve Moutria from *Torah Family*, is cutting pieces of red colored paper and taping them to our doorposts for the night of Passover. It is a great idea and learning tool for little children. I view this as a very intimate meal. It is eaten at sundown, and you are not to go outside the door of your house until morning. It would be a big sleepover event if you had a Passover party or assembly dinner for you and your friends.

Also, if you are not physically circumcised, you can't partake of the lamb. I don't want to be the one who checks everyone at a big event for that requirement. However, as we are doing this in memorial and not strict observance, this requirement may not be a sticking point. I would, however, encourage you to become circumcised as an outward declaration of your circumcised heart (If your heart is circumcised.).

Exodus 12:8 *And they shall eat the flesh in that night, roast with fire, and unleavened bread; and*

145

with bitter herbs they shall eat it.

The Bible doesn't specify what bitter herbs are. My family cooks up kale and spinach with apple cider vinegar. Some people eat horseradish or Romaine lettuce as well. Although the reason isn't given, there is a longstanding belief it is to represent the bitterness of slavery. The unleavened bread is mentioned because Passover meal is the evening meal at the start of Unleavened Breads! Also, when the Hebrews left Egypt, they left in a hurry and were not able to take their sourdough starters used to make bread. So, until they could get the starters going again, they ate unleavened bread with their meals.

Exodus 12:11 *And thus shall ye eat it; with your loins girded, your shoes on your feet, and your staff in your hand; and ye shall eat it in haste: it is the LORD'S Passover.*

Eat quickly and be ready for when YHWH calls you to leave Egypt!

Exodus 12:24 *And ye shall observe this thing for an ordinance to thee and to thy sons for ever.*

And it shall come to pass, when ye be come to the land which the LORD will give you, according as he hath promised, that ye shall keep this service. And it shall come to pass, when your children shall say unto you, What mean ye by this service? That ye shall say, It is the sacrifice of the LORD'S Passover, who passed over the houses of the children of Israel in Egypt, when he smote the Egyptians and delivered our houses. And the people bowed the head and worshipped.

Unleavened Breads

Exodus 13:1-6 *And the LORD spake unto Moses, saying, Sanctify unto me all the firstborn, whatsoever openeth the womb among the children of Israel, both of man and of beast: it is mine. And Moses said unto the people, Remember this day, in which ye came out from Egypt, out of the house of bondage; for by strength of hand the LORD brought you out from this place: there shall no leavened bread be eaten. This day came ye out in the month Abib. And it shall be when the LORD shall bring thee into the land of the Canaanites, and the Hittites, and the Amorites, and the Hivites, and the Jebusites, which he sware unto thy fathers to give*

147

thee, a land flowing with milk and honey, that thou shalt keep this service in this month. Seven days thou shalt eat unleavened bread, and in the seventh day shall be a feast to the LORD.

This is the first real commanded feast of the year, and it starts with a week of eating flatbreads, matzo, and tortillas. There are those who hold to the belief that you must eat only matzo. I have not found the command for matzo in the Bible, just unleavened bread. You can find and test many recipes online or ask friends who have celebrated Unleavened Breads in years past. I will also put some recipes at the end of the book. Get creative, there is nothing in scripture that says you can't have a kosher marshmallow s'more as your unleavened bread for the day.

Exodus 13:7 *Unleavened bread shall be eaten seven days; and there shall no leavened bread be seen with thee, neither shall there be leaven seen with thee in all thy quarters.*

Most people bust open the cabinets a week or so before and throw out things that are made with leavening. You would be surprised how many things from food to household cleaners actually have leavening in them. But again, that is not what scripture says. One Jewish tradition has people scrubbing every corner of their house in-case someone has dropped a crumb or two, throwing out their yeast, baking soda, and baking powder or locking it away in a closet for a week.

What is leaven? **Strongs Definition שְׂאֹר sᵉ'ôr,** seh-ore'; from H7604; barm or yeast-cake (as swelling by fermentation): —leaven. (*Strong's H7604*)

Subsequently, if your yeast is inactive, don't toss it in the bin. Most of us who make our own bread buy it in bulk, and throwing it away would be a waste of money and resources. It's not to be seen. If you have it sitting out on your counter, put it away. If you feel convicted, put it in a closet or locked cabinet for the week. However, it's not commanded.

***1 Corinthians 5:1-7** It is reported commonly that there is fornication among you, and such fornication as is not so much as named among the Gentiles, that one should have his father's wife. And* *ye are puffed up, and have not rather mourned, that he that hath done this deed might be taken away from among you. For I verily, as absent in body, but present in spirit, have judged already, as though I were present, concerning him that hath so done this deed, In the name of our Lord Jesus Christ, when ye are gathered together, and my spirit, with the power of our Lord Jesus Christ, To deliver such a one unto Satan for the destruction of the flesh, that the spirit may be saved in the day of the Lord Jesus. Your glorying is not good. Know ye not that a little leaven leaveneth the whole lump? Purge out therefore the old leaven, that ye may be a new lump, as ye are unleavened. For even Christ our Passover is sacrificed for us: Therefore let us keep the feast, not with old leaven, neither with the leaven of malice and wickedness; but with the unleavened bread of sincerity and truth.*

This week is a great time to reflect on your life, actions, and thoughts. Try to recognize and remove the sin from your life. Remove the old leaven, the sin, from your ways and heart.

Exodus 13:8-10 *And thou shalt shew thy son in that day, saying, This is done because of that which* *the LORD did unto me when I came forth out of Egypt. And it shall be for a sign unto thee upon thine hand, and for a memorial between thine eyes, that the LORD'S law may be in thy mouth: for with a strong hand hath the LORD brought thee out of Egypt. Thou shalt therefore keep this ordinance in his season from year to year.*

First Fruits

Leviticus 23:9-14 *And the LORD spake unto Moses, saying,Speak unto the children of Israel, and say unto them, When ye be come into the land which I give unto you, and shall reap the harvest thereof, then ye shall bring a sheaf of the first fruits of your harvest unto the priest: And he shall wave the sheaf before the LORD, to be accepted for you: on the morrow after the sabbath the priest shall wave it. And ye shall offer that day when ye wave the sheaf an he lamb without blemish of the first year for a burnt offering unto the LORD. And the meat offering thereof shall be two tenth deals of fine flour mingled with oil, an offering made by fire unto the LORD for a sweet savour: and the drink offering thereof shall be of wine, the fourth part of an hin. And ye shall eat neither bread, nor parched corn,*

151

nor green ears, until the selfsame day that ye have brought an offering unto your God: it shall be a statute forever throughout your generations in all your dwellings.

There are a lot of churches that like to talk of First Fruits, asking for extra money outside of the 10% of your tithe. Let me ask this. Does anything in this verse say a word about money? Does tithing in the Bible say anything about money? When tithing or First Fruits are mentioned, it is usually regarding your harvest, be it beast or bounty from your fields. It also says you are to give them to the priests, so they can be sacrificed at the temple. Those animals, fruits, and veggies etc. were meant not only as a sacrifice to YHWH, but also as a way for the priests to eat, because the Levitical priests were not allowed to own land. I encourage you to look into tithing as applicable for today. Since we can't observe First Fruits as we are supposed to, we usually use it as a starting point for the feast of weeks, the countdown to Shavuot or Pentecost.

Leviticus 23:15-16 *And ye shall count unto you from the morrow after the sabbath, from the day that ye brought the sheaf of the wave offering; seven*

152

sabbaths shall be complete. Even unto the morrow after the seventh sabbath shall ye number fifty days; and ye shall offer a new meat offering unto the LORD.

Shavuot/Pentecost

Deuteronomy 16:9-11 *Count off seven weeks from the time you begin to put the sickle to the standing grain. Then celebrate the Festival of Weeks to the Lord your God by giving a freewill offering in proportion to the blessings the Lord your God has given you. And rejoice before the Lord your God at the place he will choose as a dwelling for his Name—you, your sons and daughters, your male and female servants, the Levites in your towns, and the foreigners, the fatherless and the widows living among you.*

Act 2:1-6 *And when the day of Pentecost was fully come, they were all with one accord in one place. And suddenly there came a sound from heaven as of a rushing mighty wind, and it filled all the house where they were sitting. And there appeared unto them cloven tongues like as of fire, and it sat upon each of them. And they were all* *filled with the Holy Ghost, and began to speak with other tongues, as the Spirit gave them utterance. And there were dwelling at Jerusalem Jews, devout men, out of every nation under heaven. Now when this was noised abroad, the multitude came together, and were confounded, because that every man heard them speak in his own language.*

This is one of the three main pilgrimage feasts. Hebrews were to go to Jerusalem and worship and celebrate together at the temple. Since we do not have a temple in Jerusalem, how can we observe in remembrance? There aren't many teachings on this, so I will put some suggestions that I have found.

The first way to celebrate actually starts fifty days prior to this day on First Fruits. You are commanded to count the Omer. You could make an advent calendar for this and recite this in Hebrew, *"Barukh ata Adonai Eloheinu Melekh ha'Olam asher kid'shanu b'mitzvotav v'tizivanu al sefirat ha'omer."* Or in English, *"Blessed are you, our Lord our God, King of the Universe, who has sanctified us with your commandments and commanded us to count the Omer."*

This is a great opportunity to teach your children and yourself to count with Hebraic numbers! You could also use this as an opportunity to memorize favorite scripture verses daily to recite after the daily countdown. You could also learn to say, "Yeshua died for my sins, Yeshua will return"! or something of that nature in different languages to represent the languages spoken at Pentecost.

Give a "wave offering." According to the Torah, we are to bring two loaves of bread to be waved as an offering to the Lord:

Leviticus 23:17 *You shall bring from your dwelling places two loaves of bread to be waived, made of two tenths of an ephah. They shall be of fine flour, and they shall be baked with leaven, as firstfruits to the Lord.*

These two loaves of bread represent the Ten Commandments that were written down on two stone tablets. They also symbolize the Old and New testaments coming together. Have the head of house wave the two loaves of bread sometime during your own celebration. They are to be waived in every direction before YHWH as a public declaration of

His provision.

Reading the Book of Ruth is a popular tradition on Shavuot. It's also a common tradition that people have cheese plates and dishes during this day. Rich, decadent, sweet dishes are common to represent YHWH will bring us to the land flowing with milk and honey.

Although I am unsure about doing this, some people do decorate their homes with green plants and trees to represent the Tree of Eternal Life. In the next chapter, we will go over these traditions in other holiday practices, and you can make the determination for yourself if it is right for you.

Day of Trumpets/ Yom Teruah

Leviticus 23:23-25 And the LORD spoke to Moses, saying, "Speak to the people of Israel, saying, In the seventh month, on the first day of the month, you shall observe a day of solemn rest, a memorial proclaimed with blast of trumpets, a holy convocation You shall not do any ordinary work, and you shall present a food offering to the LORD."

Yom Teruah is often observed as a second new

year by Jewish observers. I would wholeheartedly object to this. Why would you celebrate a new year at the fall when everything is dying or being harvested? For that matter why do we celebrate a new year in the middle of winter? The biblical new year as commanded by YHWH is at the start of Passover month, which we previously discussed. Rosh Hashanah is likely derived by Jews incorporating Babylonian worship of false gods and holidays into their calendar and practices. Yom Teruah is commanded, but little is explained about why. With most other commanded holy days there are reasons given as to why. We can only deduce that it is in remembrance of things to come.

Ecclesiastes 1:9 *What has been is what will be, and what has been done is what will be done, and there is nothing new under the sun.*

119ministries also points out that this could be the cry of deliverance that YHWH and Yeshua will hear for the second coming. The cry for deliverance was heard to bring Israel out of Egypt. The Bible is circular, so this does make sense.

1 Thessalonians 4:16 *For the Lord himself will*

descend from heaven with a cry of command, with the voice of an archangel, and with the sound of the trumpet of God. And the dead in Christ will rise first.

Matthew 24:31 *And he shall send his angels with a great sound of a trumpet, and they shall gather together his elect from the four winds, from one end of heaven to the other.*

The walls of Jericho were brought down with shouting and the blowing of trumpets. The cry is signaling pending war, attack, and triumph.

Joshua 6:5 *And it shall come to pass, that when they make a long blast with the ram's horn, and when ye hear the sound of the trumpet, all the people shall shout with a great shout; and the wall of the city shall fall down flat, and the people shall ascend up every man straight before him.*

There are ten days between Yom Teruah and Yom Kippur (Day of Atonement). These days are commonly known as the Ten Days of Awe. These are a reminder that the Day of Atonement is coming. It is not commanded, but it is a good time to reflect on your relationship with YHWH and how you can strengthen it, because you will need it for what is coming.

Joel 2:1-5 Blow a trumpet in Zion; sound an alarm on my holy mountain! Let all the inhabitants of the land tremble, for the day of the LORD is coming; it is near, a day of darkness and gloom, a day of clouds and thick darkness! Like blackness there is spread upon the mountains a great and powerful people; their like has never been before, nor will be again after them through the years of all generations. Fire devours before them, and behind them a flame burns. The land is like the garden of Eden before them, but behind them a desolate wilderness, and nothing escapes them. Their appearance is like the appearance of horses, and like war horses they run. As with the rumbling of chariots, they leap on the tops of the mountains, like the crackling of a flame of fire devouring the stubble, like a powerful army drawn up for battle.

Day of Atonement/ Yom Kippur

Leviticus 23:26-32 And the LORD spake unto Moses, saying, Also on the tenth day of this seventh

159

month there shall be a day of atonement: it shall be an holy convocation unto you; and ye shall afflict your souls, and offer an offering made by fire unto the LORD. And ye shall do no work in that same day: for it is a day of atonement, to make an atonement for you before the LORD your God. For whatsoever soul it be that shall not be afflicted in that same day, he shall be cut off from among his people. And whatsoever soul it be that doeth any work in that same day, the same soul will I destroy from among his people. Ye shall do no manner of work: it shall be a statute forever throughout your generations in all your dwellings. It shall be unto you a sabbath of rest, and ye shall afflict your souls: in the ninth day of the month at even, from even unto even, shall ye celebrate your sabbath.

On Yom Kippur, we are not to work, or we will be destroyed. It is a commandment that is forever, no matter where we live. We are to deny and afflict ourselves from sunset to sunset. We no longer have to the sin sacrifice. As we have talked about earlier, Yeshua is our blood atonement.

__2 Corinthians 5:21__ For he hath made him to be sin for us, who knew no sin; that we might be made *the righteousness of God in him*

We are to afflict ourselves. Many people believe this means to fast. When we fast, it shows that we are not a slave to our appetites—that we place our spiritual hunger above that of our physical desires. Denying ourselves of food, sex or other things our body desires, brings us to a better understanding of what Yeshua was tempted with for forty days in the desert. Yeshua said a man does not live on bread alone but on every word that comes from the Father.

Afflicting our souls also means that we are to humble ourselves before the Father. By bowing down, we show we are submitting to His authority over us and our lives. We realize that He is the one true God, and that the only way to Him is through accepting Yeshua as Messiah by repenting and turning from our sins.

It is a commonly held belief in Torah observance that Yeshua has completed the first half of the feasts in his first coming, as I outlined earlier, and that he will come back fulfilling that last half. If He comes back on Yom Teruah with the blasting of trumpets, the world will have ten days to repent and return to YHWH. Yom Kippur is the day of judgment. On that day, when we are judged, we probably will not be feeling much like eating.

Zechariah 14:12 And this shall be the plague with which the LORD will strike all the peoples that wage war against Jerusalem: their flesh will rot while they are still standing on their feet, their eyes will rot in their sockets, and their tongues will rot in their mouths.

This verse alone gives me less than a healthy appetite after reading it. I cannot imagine what actually seeing it in person would do to someone, especially knowing that some of those people will be loved ones and friends who did not listen to the truth when it was presented to them.

I do understand that some people cannot fast for health reasons. If possible fast, but do not endanger yourself. Afflict yourself in other ways—do a fast of Facebook, compute,r or television. Talk to your doctor to see if you could intermittently fast for the day without hurting yourself. The whole point of the day is to reflect and purge yourself of sin. You feed your spirit and strengthen your relationship and understanding of YHWH.

Feast of Tabernacles/ Sukkot

Leviticus 23:33-43 And the LORD spoke to Moses, saying, "Speak to the people of Israel, saying, On the fifteenth day of this seventh month and for seven days is the Feast of Booths to the LORD. On the first day shall be a holy convocation; you shall not do any ordinary work. For seven days you shall present food offerings to the LORD. On the eighth day you shall hold a holy convocation and present a food offering to the LORD. It is a solemn assembly; you shall not do any ordinary work. These are the appointed feasts of the LORD, which you shall proclaim as times of holy convocation, for presenting to the LORD food offerings, burnt offerings and grain offerings, sacrifices and drink offerings, each on its proper day, besides the LORD's Sabbaths and besides your gifts and besides all your vow offerings and besides all your freewill offerings, which you give to the LORD. On the fifteenth day of the seventh month, when you have gathered in the produce of the land, you shall celebrate the feast of the LORD seven days. On the first day shall be a solemn rest, and on the eighth day shall be a solemn rest. And you shall take on the first day the fruit of splendid trees, branches of palm trees and boughs of leafy trees and willows of the brook, and you shall rejoice before the LORD your God seven days. You shall celebrate it as a feast to the LORD for seven days in the year. It is a statute forever throughout your generations; you shall celebrate it in the seventh month. You shall dwell in booths for seven days. All native Israelites shall dwell in booths, that your generations may know that I made the people of Israel dwell in booths when I brought them out of the land of Egypt: I am the LORD your God."

Some people would argue that because this states it is for the native-born Israelites, we cannot observe it. I would like to remind those people that in Numbers 15:15, we are grafted in and are a part of Israel. Therefore, we are commanded to celebrate this week with joy! This week we are to fellowship, celebrate, and memorialize the Exodus of the people of Israel from the bondage of Egypt. We are commanded to take part of our tithes and put it towards this event to purchase whatever our hearts lust after (within Torah Law, of course).

This has to be one of the most anticipated holy days in the calendar. It's a time for celebration, fellowship, and making friends—a commanded week-long party! How great is that?! Most people take the week off from work. If you can't though, that is ok. Just note that there are two commanded rest days in this event. Beginning and end of the week are days that need to be taken off, if at all possible.

This Holy week is when we all dust off our camping gear and rough it. Some people rough it in campers or cabins, but the command is a sukkah. Weather permitting sleeping in a booth with no roof may be possible. But as Sukkot is in the fall and most areas in America are not conducive to literal under the stars camping, tents are the answer! For those who aren't able to go to a Sukkot event, backyard camping is an awesome fun thing for you and the kids. I know of a few people who medically can't leave their homes. So, they make mini tents on their couches and beds so that they are still in a sukkah.

As of the writing of this chapter, my family and I have only been able to observe at home. We set up a tent in the house or the backyard and observe family time and meals in it. Those lucky people who get to go fellowship with others spend the week learning new skills. Some events have lectures or presentations on biblical things. Some focus on survival or camping skills. Depending on your level on comfort, you can try roughing it in some areas that are completely without electricity or plumbing. You can learn realistic, effective, homesteading and survival skills.

This is a memorial of the time when the Hebrews were brought out of Egypt, a time of great joy for the people of YHWH. This is also prophetic of things that will come. It is no secret that there will be a time that we as believers will need to escape and hide in the coming tribulation. We will be camping, roughing it, and on the move to stay alive. Sukkot is an excellent way to practice these skills. Muscle memory and ingrained knowledge of how to start and cook on a fire, hunt for wild edibles, or butcher your own food, and how to set up a tent etc., are essential to survival in a lot of different situations.

This feast of tabernacles is also prophetic of the Wedding Feast.

Revelation 19:7 *Let us be glad and rejoice, and give honour to him: for the marriage of the Lamb is come, and his wife hath made herself ready. And to her was granted that she should be arrayed in fine linen, clean and white: for the fine linen is the righteousness of saints. And he saith unto me, Write, Blessed are they which are called unto the marriage supper of the Lamb. And he saith unto me, These are the true sayings of God.*

If Yeshua comes back on Trumpet and passes judgment on Atonement, it is only logical to believe that the week-long, commanded, joyful celebration will be the wedding supper spoken of in Revelations. Those of us who have followed the instructions of the Father and Yeshua will be the bride, and those who are least of the kingdom will be the guests.

ARE THE HOLIDAYS HOLY?

Deuteronomy 12:1 *"These are the statutes and rules that you shall be careful to do in the land that the LORD, the God of your fathers, has given you to possess, all the days that you live on the earth. You shall surely destroy all the places where the nations whom you shall dispossess served their gods, on the high mountains and on the hills and under every green tree. You shall tear down their altars and dash in pieces their pillars and burn their Asherim with fire. You shall chop down the carved images of their gods and destroy their name out of that place. You shall not worship the LORD your God in that way.*

So, you've made it through the whole book, and now you have reached this chapter. It's probably going to be the hardest one to accept. I am disputing the very core of most of our fondest memories and traditions. For many, these holidays hold feelings of warmth and love, and that is wonderful. But this book is to talk about how YHWH wants you to love Him—not about how you want to love Him. The truth of the matter is that many of us practice these traditions and observe these days out of ignorance—out of lack of knowledge. Thinking that you are honoring YHWH or Yeshua in these ways without knowing what they really stand for, will not be an acceptable excuse. Remember, the Bible warns that people will perish for lack of knowledge.

Hosea 4:6 My people are destroyed for lack of knowledge; because you have rejected knowledge, I reject you from being a priest to me. And since you have forgotten the law of your God, I also will forget your children.

Grab a pen and paper and take notes, so you can fact check them yourself. I am going to go over the most observed and popular "Christian" and secular holidays on the calendar. The fact of the matter is, you cannot "Christianize" something meant for the worship of Pagan gods. You cannot worship YHWH in a way that He says is wrong and expect it to be acceptable to Him. The cold truth is that the

Catholic/Christian church has mutated and stolen Pagan traditions, holidays, and practices and tried to slap a cross on them, claiming them as their own. This, I believe, is one of the things YHWH was talking about in Isaiah, as we discussed earlier in the book. You can try to argue away the facts. You can dismiss the truth for what it is by saying, "That's not what it means to me." However, if you go back to the story of the golden calf in Exodus and really read it, you will see that some of the Israelites made the same mistake and paid dearly for it. It's not about what it means to you. It is about what it means to HIM.

New Year

This holiday never made sense to me. Why in the world did a new year start in the middle of winter? But I got out of school and work on that day, so who was I to sit down and really think? New Year's Eve is a world-wide event. The countdown begins, and people start looking for a face to suck on at midnight. People get crazy drunk and make poor, reckless decisions to embrace the new year with regret and a hangover. The next day they sip on their coffee and try to forget (if they remember) the night before and have a New Year's meal of abomination sausage and sauerkraut. But where does this day come from?

Exo 12:1 The LORD said to Moses and Aaron in the land of Egypt "This month shall be for you the beginning of months. It shall be the first month of the year for you. Tell all the congregation of Israel that on the tenth day of this month every man shall take a lamb according to their fathers' houses, a lamb for a household.

We can determine from this passage that the new year is intended to be in the spring before Passover meal. So, why January? It can be traced back to the Roman god, Janus. The whole month of January was named for him. He is the two-faced god of gateways, said to be able to look into the future and the past. During this month people would decorate their homes with laurels and throw raunchy parties. They would sacrifice animals to him in hopes of gaining good fortune. People would exchange gifts and well wishes. "Happy New Year!" is a well wish. It's a Pagan practice for the observation of this day (Note: not all well wishes are Pagan false god worship.). At many points

172

throughout history, the observation of this day was abolished. The last time by the Council of Tours, but the practice of gift exchanged was moved to December twenty-fifth. However, Pope Gregory XIII re-established it, and the Gregorian calendar was adopted by the Catholic church and the world around 1600 BC.

The tradition of eating pork and sauerkraut all in itself is steeped in superstition. This is a Germanic tradition. It is believed that because pigs lack the ability to turn their heads and look behind them, it is good luck to eat them. The sauerkraut is shredded, and it is believed that the number of shreds of the cabbage is the amount of money you will get in the upcoming year. So not only are you eating an animal the YHWH has deemed unclean, you are eating something with the thought of greed for money in your heart. The observation of New Year as a holiday or a day to be celebrated is not biblical. It is Pagan in its very nature. Yes, we still must change the date on our checks and paperwork, because we are under the Gregorian calendar. But we do not have to celebrate this Pagan day with parties and superstitions.

Valentine's Day

Oh, how I dislike this holiday! I have for as long as I can remember. The commercialization and money that are wasted on this day is nauseating. People, on average, spend over eighteen billion dollars or more on these empty gestures. Why do people designate one day to show someone that you love them? Because some executive somewhere decided that they could make money from people by slapping some hearts and a cherub on a box. Aside from the disgusting commercialized aspects of this day, is it biblical, or at the very least, not against the Bible?

Colossians 2:8 *See to it that no one takes you captive by philosophy and empty deceit, according to human tradition, according to the elemental spirits of the world, and not according to Christ.*

Valentine's day is often represented as a day remembering St. Valentine, a man who would perform illegal marriages during the time of Christian persecution when the Romans made marriage illegal. The law at the time was that only single men could serve in the military service of

174

Rome. There were not enough unmarried men to draft. He was said to have been martyred on February 14th. He was named the patron saint of true love. This is obvious idol worship. But all in all, this version doesn't seem too bad. In fact, it seems very sweet, romantic, and Christian.

This isn't where the traditions or practices really come from. Valentine's day is the Christianization of Lupercalia, a Roman festival in celebration of the wolf, Lupercus. The myth is that Romulus and Remus were sentenced to die by their uncle, the Emperor, as a punishment to his sister, their mother, for breaking her vow of chastity. The maids who were tasked with this deed took pity on them and placed them in a basket and set it in the river (that sounds familiar...). The basket got tangled in some weeds, and the boys were found by the wolf, Lupercus. The wolf then nursed them until they were found and adopted by a shepherd and his wife. When the boys got older, they killed their uncle and declared a day of worship and celebration of the wolf who saved them.

This was a three-day festival in February, the thirteenth thru the fifteenth. This was also a fertility

175

ritual. Men would sacrifice goats and dogs while naked, making whips from the hides and would go around beating women with them. The women would actually line up to get hit! They would also put women's names in a jar, and men would then draw out a name. They would couple for, at minimum, the duration of the festival, sometimes ending in marriage. This can now be seen in partial practice today in many elementary schools with the building of Valentine's Day card boxes.

The Luperci were Roman priests who would pick two men to stand naked while they made a sacrifice to Lupercus. The naked men would stand while blood from the knife was smeared on their foreheads. The blood was removed at the end of the festival with a goat hide dipped in goat's milk. The first thing that popped into my mind while reading this was Exodus 23:19. Whether or not the command was pertaining to this practice or not, I do not know. I just thought it was interesting to note the connection.

The date of February fourteenth is also linked to the Greek god, Juno as a festival day for her. The pagan god, Pan, who is actually Baphomet, is also linked to this festival through the goats. Pan was a god of lust, fertility, and a host of other things. He would have sex with anything, but seemed to favor goats.

The symbolism used during this day is Pagan in origin as well. Cupid is always associated with Valentine's Day—the cute little-winged angel shooting his love into everyone's heart. Biblically speaking, angels that have interacted with humans do not have wings. They come in the form of man. The only time angels were spoken about with wings they were in the heavenly realm. Cupid stems again from Pagan worship. He is a Greek god of desire, erotic love, attraction, and affection. In other words, lust, and nothing of the pure love between a man and a woman that is gifted by YHWH. He is not an angel. He is a false god and a demon.

The heart shape in and of itself is not bad. Given the connection to this holiday and Cupid one can assume in this context, it is. It may actually be linked to an extinct heart-shaped herb silphium, which was believed to be an ancient form of contraception and an abortifacient. That's exactly what it sounds like, the world's first abortion pill.

So, when you see Cupid with his heart, he is promising lust and sex without consequences. If you feel you need a day to dedicate to your love, don't do it on Pagan days in Pagan ways.

St. Patrick's Day

I have to admit that when I did the research for this one, I was surprised. When you think of St. Patty's day, images of green beer, leprechauns, and drunken idiots fill the mind. As someone who comes from Irish ancestry, I always thought this was stereotypical ignorance. It is, but the Irish pander to it for monetary gain and tourism.

Saint Patrick's Day is actually disliked by most generational witches that come from Ireland. It is in honor of Saint Patrick. He is responsible for driving out the Pagan practices and false god worship from Ireland. The story says snakes. But as snakes are not indigenous to Ireland, it is actually a euphemism for Pagans. The four-leaf clover actually started as a three leaf and was a symbol of the Holy Trinity. When he died on March seventeenth, the Pope declared it a day of remembrance and solemn observance. Still idol worship, but how it morphed into the drunken debauchery that is it today no one knows. Today's version of the day is smothered in Paganism.

The original color of Saint Patrick's Day was actually blue. Blue is often found in the Bible. We are required to run a cord of blue through our tzitzits. But it was changed to green after the 1798 Irish resistance to the British invasion.

Leprechauns are mischievous fairies that are said to be shoe cobblers who hoard their pay at the end of rainbows. Fairies and Fae are linked to Nephilim and fallen angels. They are not creatures of imagination. They are not kind, and they are not from YHWH. In fact, this particular creature is a protected species in the EU. These little demons inspire greed in the hearts of man. It is said, if you catch one, they will grant you three wishes and give you their gold in exchange for release.

I am not sure why, but the Blarney stone is often associated with this day as well. The Blarney stones origins are surrounded in mystery. The caretakers of the stone believe that it was brought to Ireland by a witch who clung to it and used its powers to save

179

herself from drowning. It's said that if you kiss it you will be gifted eloquent speech. It is not something a Christian should associate with. Hundreds of people line up daily to lay on their backs, hold on to a bar, and kiss this rock. That's gross and unhygienic. It's a superstition and a dangerous one considering you can catch a communicable disease from it.

Mardi Gras

Mardi Gras is an event that is celebrated throughout the world. It is usually a two-week celebration of over-indulgence and sin before the start of Lent. Mardi Gras itself is one day, Fat Tuesday right before Ash Wednesday. It is always forty-seven days before Easter, so the dates change yearly. There is no disputing that it is steeped in sin and not of YHWH. But it has been allowed and ordained by that Catholic church, so we will discuss it. Mardi Gras is not only Pagan to its roots, but it is also very dangerous. Women are sexually assaulted. There are fights, kidnappings, and even murders.

Mardi Gras started well before the Roman Catholics adopted it and its customs. It is linked to

Lupercalia, which we have discussed and Saturnalia, which we will discuss later in the chapter. It interesting to note that it has its own god. Dionysus/ Bacchus is the god of revelry. People who go to Mardi Gras are often called revelers. What is the definition of revelry?

STRONGS Definition of revelry: κῶμος κῶμος, κωμου, ὁ (from κεῖμαι; accordingly equivalent to German Gelag; cf. Curtius, § 45); from (Homer h. Merc., Theognis) Herodotus down; a revel, carousel, i. e. in the Greek writings properly, a nocturnal and riotous procession of half drunken and frolicsome fellows who after supper parade through the streets with torches and music in honor of Bacchus or some other deity, and sing and play before the houses of their male and female friends; hence, used generally, of feasts and drinking parties that are protracted till late at night and indulge in revelry (*Strong's 2970*)

Galatians 5:19 *Now the works of the flesh are manifest, which are these; Adultery, fornication, uncleanness, lasciviousness, Idolatry, witchcraft, hatred, variance, emulations, wrath, strife, seditions, heresies, Envyings, murders,*

*drunkenness, revellings, and such like: of the which
I tell you before, as I have also told you in time
past, that they which do such things shall not inherit
the kingdom of God.*

That sounds like an exact description of Mardi
Gras. I could probably stop right there and move on
to lent, but I feel it's important to drive the point
home. Mardi Gras, even though it's ordained as a
religious holiday, is also one of the more popular
homosexual events. If you go to Mardi Gras, you
will see homosexuality on full display. You will see
naked women and men masturbating or having sex
in full view of the public. Women flash their bare
breasts for cheap beads. The color of the beads has
specific meaning as well—purple for justice, green
for faith, and gold for power. Now either these
women exposing themselves for beads are in the
worship of a false god promising these things, or it's
in mockery of YHWH and what He offers. Either
way, it is sinful and disturbing.

The maypole is connected to Baal worship.
That's right the same one mentioned in the Bible.

The masks stem from the fallen angels. They

could be trying to look like false gods. They could also be trying to hide themselves from the judgment of YHWH and others, so they can commit their sins and debauchery in public with autonomy.

The parade starts off with a giant float that is a smoke-breathing dragon. People in the parade are literally following a creature that is known as a symbol of Satan in the Bible. The goat man in the parade is a salute to Pan/ Baphomet. It may be some old goat herder on the float, but the only thing ever titled, "goat man," was Baphomet. The cake is from the Pagan holiday Cake Day, where cakes were baked in honor of the dead.

This is ordained and sometimes even promoted by the Catholic church. It is almost like they are saying to indulge in all the sin that you know is against YHWH for a bit before you have to give it up for forty days. That is not in the Bible anywhere. We are to turn from our sins and not look back, not wallow in them like a pig in the muck!

Ash Wednesday

Ash Wednesday is a day that Catholics go to

church, line up for a blessing, and have a smudge of ash rubbed on their foreheads. It's a day of fasting. Interesting to note that this is actually a Hindu tradition used in the worship of a fire god. The ashes are called the seed of Agni, and they smudge the ashes over their third eye chakra. It was also an ancient Nordic belief that if you wore ashes on your forehead, you would receive the protection of Odin. Also consider the connection of the Luperci ceremony. Wherever the practice comes from, it is nowhere in the Bible and is not ordained by YHWH.

Matthew 6:16-18 *Moreover when ye fast, be not, as the hypocrites, of a sad countenance: for they disfigure their faces, that they may appear unto men to fast. Verily I say unto you, They have their reward. But thou, when thou fastest, anoint thine head, and wash thy face; That thou appear not unto men to fast, but unto thy Father which is in secret: and thy Father, which seeth in secret, shall reward thee openly.*

Lent

Lent is forty-six days before Easter. It is an

observance of the Catholic church. You give up things, food, possessions, addictions like smoking etc. It's also called the Great Fast. We are not commanded to fast in the Bible with the possible exception of Yom Teruah. Even though Yeshua was in the desert for forty days, fasting and fighting temptation, we are not commanded to do this. According to the Catholic church, the aim is to purify us from our sins so that we will be ready for the coming of Christ. The Bible says the only way to get into heaven or be saved of sin, is through the blood of Yeshua, not rituals or works. The church may claim this as the reasoning for Lent, but let's dig a bit deeper. Since almost every holiday we have discussed thus far has been nothing more than the adoption of Pagan practices by the church, one could make the argument this one is too.

Colossians 2:20 Wherefore if ye be dead with Christ from the rudiments of the world, why, as though living in the world, are ye subject to ordinances. (Touch not; taste not; handle not; Which all are to perish with the using;) after the commandments and doctrines of men? Which things have indeed a shew of wisdom in will worship, and

185

*humility, and neglecting of the body; not in any
honour to the satisfying of the flesh?*

"The forty days' abstinence of Lent was
borrowed from the worshippers of the Babylonian
goddess Ashtoreth/ Astarte/Ishtar. Such a Lent of
forty days, in the spring of the year, is still observed
by the Yezidis or pagan Devil-worshippers of
Koordistan, who have inherited it from their early
masters, the Babylonians. Such a Lent of forty days
was held in spring by the Pagan Mexicans. Such a
Lent of forty days was observed in Egypt." *(Hislop,
The Two Babylons, pp. 104, 105)*

Lent was initiated three hundred years after the
crucifixion of Yeshua. Nevertheless, the practice of
fasting for forty days can be traced back to the
Babylonian mourning ritual of the god, Tammuz, or
as he was known in Egypt, Osiris. In fact, it was
spoken about in Ezekiel.

Ezekiel 8:14-15 *Then he brought me to the door
of the gate of the LORD'S house which was toward
the north; and, behold, there sat women weeping for
Tammuz. Then said he unto me, Hast thou seen this,
O son of man? turn thee yet again, and thou shalt*

see greater abominations than these.

Tammuz was said to have been born of a virgin mother. He was married to the goddess, Ishtar/Eostre/Ostara, who was said to be the queen of heaven. He was a hunter who was killed by a boar. His followers mourn and fast for forty days, and at the end have a feast of pig. Easter ham anyone?

April Fool's Day

This is mostly passed over by anyone who has reached a maturity level beyond middle school. However, some people really celebrate and enjoy this day. It stemmed from when the Council of Trent started following the Gregorian calendar. Because the news was slow moving, many people still celebrated the new year at its rightful time at the start of spring, and the people of France decided that they would poke fun at those backward people by taping a paper fish to them. Now, this seems fairly innocent. However, I would ask you to think. Who would still be celebrating the new year in the spring long enough for the Poisson d'Avril (April fish) to become a tradition? One would think by the end of the first or second year, everyone would know the calendar was changed. It is known that followers of Yeshua used the symbol of a fish to notify others who they were during the persecution of Christians. I would speculate that this was a sinister way to ostracized and humiliate those who still followed the Torah. To me, it is very reminiscent of the yellow stars used by the Nazi's during their persecution of the Jews. Harmless fun or something worse?

Easter

Easter has been passed down throughout the generations as the day that Yeshua was resurrected. Sunrise services and church events run the gambit from simple lunches to Easter egg hunts. It's taught to us that Yeshua was crucified on Good Friday and rose from the grave on Easter. What did Yeshua say about the time frame of this event?

Matthew 12:40 *For as Jonas was three days and three nights in the whale's belly; so shall the Son of man be three days and three nights in the heart of the earth.*

Three days and three nights—let's do a little math—Friday Day/ Friday Night (1) Saturday Day/ Saturday Night (2) Sunday Day (He Rises). That does not add up. We know that Mary started out for Yeshua's tomb on the first day of the week and started out while it was still dark. Well, a Hebrew day actually starts in the evening. If you look at the holy days, they all start in the evening. YHWH walked with Adam and Eve in the evening, at the start of the day.

John 20:1 *The first day of the week cometh Mary Magdalene early, when it was yet dark, unto the sepulchre, and seeth the stone taken away from the sepulchre.*

So, Yeshua rose on a Saturday night. Three days and three nights before that would have placed his crucifixion on the ninth hour on a Wednesday. They wanted him off the cross before sunset, because the High Sabbath of Unleavened Breads was going to start at sundown. That would give Mary enough time Friday during the day to purchase the herbs to anoint Yeshua on the evening after the Sabbath.

Besides the now obvious mathematical

189

improbability of an Easter sunrise resurrection, what else is completely wrong about this day? — everything. Even the name is an English version of Eostre who is also known as Ostra. The Council of Nicaea decided to fix the day on the first Sunday after the full moon of the vernal equinox. This is yet another theft of Pagan observances.

MAR. 20 or 21: OSTARA SABBAT: Spring Equinox; The Goddess of Spring. Spring Equinox aka Vernal Equinox aka Ostara, marks the beginning of Spring. Days and nights are exactly equal, the sun rises and sets in the exact east and west. This holiday represents the first creation, but also the annual creation (planting so crops grow each year) and most symbolic, the perpetual creation. Fertility symbols abound such as eggs and rabbits. Spring or Vernal Equinox begins a forty-day period which culminates with May Day, another fertility Spring festival of ancient origin. "Pagan Calendar of Observances", accessed 1/28/2019 www.wftacademyofpaganstudies.org/our-schedules-calendars/pagan-calendar-of-observances/

When you go to a sunrise service, you are not celebrating the resurrection of Yeshua. You are actually worshiping the sun and paying homage to Ostra.

The eggs that our children hunt stem from many different Pagan traditions or beliefs. It is believed that Ostra healed a wounded bird by changing it into a hare. Because it still was partially a bird, it would hop around laying eggs to show gratitude to Ostra. In ancient Egypt, the egg symbolizes the sun. In ancient Babylon, it was worshiped because it was believed that Ishtar was hatched from one when she fell from heaven. Aside from the bunny bird of Ostra, rabbits were used in fertility rituals, because well, they are bunnies. The euphemism is used for a reason, people.

Most people celebrate their Easter dinner with a big spread that includes an Easter ham. Like I mentioned in the information about Lent, a boar killed Ostara's husband, Tammuz, and following the forty days of mourning they end the celebration by killing a pig and eating it. We all know that ham

191

is an abomination in the eyes of YHWH. I cannot imagine how He would feel to know an abomination is eaten in a false celebration to supposedly honor the sacrifice Yeshua made.

<u>Halloween</u>

This one is met with mixed opinions among the Christian community. There are some who abhor the day and have nothing to do with it. Others have Trunk or Treat, Halloween parties only for members of their church or some other similar concession. A lot of us do not want our children to feel singled out or picked on because of our beliefs. Unfortunately, that excuse will not pass muster on the day of judgment. I am a mother. I have three children and two of them have celebrated Halloween and all the fun that entails with it. Had I known what I know now, I would not have passed that tradition on to them. I repent and mourn for this.

Halloween is also known as Samhain and All Hallows Day. Samhain was started by the Celts. They believed that the veil between our world and the world of the dead is at its thinnest at this time. The custom of wearing costumes was started to ward off ghosts. Trick or Treating was implemented in the sixteenth century, in Scotland. Children would go around dressed as the dead to receive offerings on behalf of the ghosts. They also believed that dressing as the ghost would protect them from an attack and help to blend in with them.

Jack o' Lanterns actually started out as turnips. They were carved to represent or ward off evil spirits. It wasn't until later that it was changed to pumpkins, because it was believed the smell of pumpkin warded off vampires.

People would go to druids during this time because of the veil being thin thinking they could get predictions for the future or speak to long-dead relatives. Apples and roasting nuts were also used for the purpose of dream interpretation as well. Women would mark apples with their mark, and men would bob for them. It was believed that this was a foretelling of whom the women would marry.

Exodus 22:18 *Thou shalt not suffer a witch to live.*

Deuteronomy 18:10-11 *There shall not be*

found among you any one that maketh his son or his daughter to pass through the fire, or that useth divination, or an observer of times, or an enchanter, or a witch, Or a charmer, or a consulter with familiar spirits, or a wizard, or a necromancer. For all that do these things are an abomination unto the LORD: and because of these abominations the LORD thy God doth drive them out from before thee.

How many times have we or someone we loved dressed up as a witch, zombie, vampire, werewolf, or a character from Harry Potter? How often do we go into a palm reader or a psychic on Halloween just for the experience? A cat is often known as a witch's familiar. A bowed-up, hissing, black cat is a common part of the decor. How often have we had our kids dress up as a cute kitty, or dressed up as one ourselves? These things are an abomination in the eyes of YHWH, and we have pandered to the practices for the sake of inclusion.

The days around Halloween are when the FBI sees an uptick in cases of kidnapping, murder, and animal sacrifices. Satanic cults still sacrifice humans and animals to Satan. I encourage you to investigate Satanic Ritual Abuse and the FBI statistics about this day.

Did you know that Anton Lavey founded the Church of Satan on Halloween? He did so because it is a high holy day for those who worship the devil. It is considered a self-centered holiday to them, because you are exploring your inner self through costume. Isn't that the big belief about the trans community? That they are just being who they feel they are on the inside? Quoting Anton, "This night, we smile at amateur explorers of their inner darkness. We enjoy their indulgence and dress up of our practices even if it's only once a year. Anytime during the rest of the year that they point out our practices we can point to their hypocritical observance of this day." It was also told from a former devil worshiper that Anton said "I am glad Christians let their children worship the devil at least once a year. Welcome to Halloween." John Ramerez, accessed 01/29/2019 https://www1.cbn.com/cbnnews/us/2017/october/fo rmer-satanist-warns-christians-about-celebrating-halloween

If a day is supported, endorsed, and celebrated

by Satanists, you can safely assume that it is not in any way a holiday supported by YHWH.

Christmas

Oh, how I have dreaded writing this part of the chapter- The Sacred Cow of Christianity. Most open-minded believers are agreeable, or at least tolerant of, Torah Observant followers until this topic comes up. Then they are hit by the Spirit of Christmas, and they become downright abusive. People will completely shut down when you start to dismantle the traditions of Christmas. They will defend this day to their dying breath. Unfortunately, everything about this day is Pagan, including the day itself. A very famous televangelist was asked about Christmas being Pagan, and he admitted it was. He then dismissed the truth by stating that we "Christianized" it. As we have already established, YHWH doesn't want "Christianized" Pagan traditions in His name. He wants those things destroyed with extreme prejudice. Therefore, let's just rip the band-aid off, shall we?

Yeshua was not born on December 25th. Researchers have deduced, based on Biblical context, that He was born sometime around The Feast of Tabernacles, probably September eleventh. That day should ring a few bells and bring up questions, but that's for a different author. The god that was born on December twenty-fifth was none other than Nimrod (*The Two Babylons*, referenced on page 189 of this chapter, actually traces all false gods to Nimrod and his wife/mother.).

Christmas is linked to the Roman holiday, Saturnalia. This was to honor, Saturn, the god of agriculture, who was also born on December twenty-fifth. Saturnalia was considered the most sacred day of the year. These worshipers believed that the sun god was sick and weak every winter and would celebrate the solstice, because it meant that he was getting well again. They would decorate their homes with evergreen boughs. They believed that those boughs also warded off witches, ghosts, evil spirits, and illness.

Christmas trees are linked to multiple Pagan rituals and beliefs. Romans would bring in pines, spruce, evergreens, or fir trees into their homes every winter. It reminded them that the sun god was going to get better, and the green things would grow again, and summer would return. The Egyptians would use palm rushes as a type of worship for RA as a symbol of triumph over death. Druids believed the evergreen was a symbol of everlasting life. Vikings believed that evergreens were a special plant of the sun god, Babler. In Norse tradition, decorating the tree was done to represent a family god or deity. The Norse would also hang a wreath to honor Odin. "Oh, Christmas tree, Oh Christmas tree how lovely are your branches..".

__Jeremiah 10:3__ For the customs of the people are vain: for one cutteth a tree out of the forest, the work of the hands of the workman, with the axe. They deck it with silver and with gold; they fasten it with nails and with hammers, that it move not. They are upright as the palm tree, but speak not: they must needs be borne, because they cannot go. Be not afraid of them; for they cannot do evil, neither also is it in them to do good.

The Yule Log is from the Norse people bringing huge logs into their homes and town halls. They would burn them for a feast and exchange gifts. That could take as long as twelve days. Hence, the song, Twelve Days of Christmas. They also believed that each spark was a representation of a pig or a calf that would be born to them in the coming year.

Caroling is something that I have not personally done or seen in person. Surprisingly, people still do participate in this. Caroling actually stems from fertility rites and rituals. Villagers traveled through fields and orchards in the middle of winter singing and shouting to drive away the spirits that might hinder growth.

Mistletoe has long been considered a magical plant. Romans would hold fertility rituals under the mistletoe. Get that out of your head the next time granny meets you under the mistletoe for a smooch. The Norse would meet under the mistletoe and lay down their arms in honor of the goddess, Frigga.

Decking the halls is not as pure as one would think. The holly leaf is a symbol of the Norse god of winter, the Holly King. He would battle with the Oak King. It was also believed to ward off evil. In ancient Egypt and during Saturnalia, vines or boughs of holly were used to decorate and ward off winter evils. "Deck the halls with boughs of Holly,

FaLa Lala La..."

Gingerbread men are a sweeter version of the human sacrifices burned alive during Saturnalia and the Norse winter sacrifices.

Santa Claus, while made popular by Coca-Cola marketing geniuses, stems from a culmination of many different beliefs. If you look up old nick online or in the dictionary, it says it is Satan. The Catholics state that Saint Nick is the reason for Santa Claus. The Norse told their children that Odin, who Santa resembles, would watch them while they slept and would punish those who misbehaved. The Italian witch, La Befana, would leave gifts and treats to good children during their winter celebration. And Frau Holle gave gifts to women at the winter solstice.

There are many, who upon finding out that Santa Claus, the tooth fairy, and the Easter bunny are lies, start to question the authenticity of Yeshua. We are commanded not to lie. We tell our children over and over again not to lie. We punish them for it, and yet, every year in the name of fun we lie to our children over and over. Then when they start to hide things from us, we wonder why they do not trust us!

These holidays are nothing more than repackaged worship of false gods—repackaged worship of the devil meant to trick those with real love in their hearts for YHWH and Yeshua into breaking His commandments and breaking His heart. Many ministers know the truth, but say that if they were to stop Easter and Christmas worships, they would lose their churches. It's become more important to them to pander to people than tell the truth. If I brought you a piece of dog poop shaped in a square and covered in frosting, would you call it a brownie and eat it? We as believers are not meant to blend in with the doings of this world. We are not to hide our lights under a bushel for fear of being different. We are to be set apart. The Bible warns we will be persecuted for His name's sake. Why would we be persecuted if we are doing the exact same thing that everyone else does, even if in our minds it's for different reasons?

THE NARROW PATH ... A WARNING

> ***Matthew 7:14*** *Because strait is the gate, and narrow is the way, which leadeth unto life, and few there be that find it.*

I am writing this chapter for two reasons. One is to warn you that now that you know the truth of how to speak YHWH's love language, if you chose to ignore, it then you are guilty of rebellion. As we researched, rebellion is what caused Israel to be kicked out in the first place. So please pray over what you have read and search out the scriptures before you turn your back on the truth. Don't take my, or anyone else's word for it. Open your Bible and do the research yourself! If nothing else, I pray it brings you to the understanding of those of us who believe this is the truth of how YHWH wants us to love Him. Once again, I want to reiterate. *You do not follow the law for salvation. You follow the law as a fruit of your salvation.* You follow the law because you love YHWH and Yeshua. If you want to speak Their love language, if you want to be set apart in the world as commanded, then follow the law. It is true that there are some laws that we cannot follow or observe completely, for one reason or another. But we are TRYING, and that is what matters. We are not reading the words and just tossing them aside, because if we can't follow them fully, we might as well not follow them at all. We are not creating our own ways to worship. We are trying our very best to follow YHWH and Yeshua as they commanded.

Matthew 7:21-23 *"Not everyone who says to me, 'Lord, Lord,' will enter the kingdom of heaven, but the one who does the will of my Father who is in heaven. On that day many will say to me, 'Lord, Lord, did we not prophesy in your name, and cast out demons in your name, and do many mighty works in your name?' And then will I declare to them, 'I never knew you; depart from me, you workers of lawlessness.'*

Yes, once saved always saved. The Bible clearly and repeatedly states that for you to be saved, you must accept Yeshua and follow his commandments. If you don't, are you truly saved? There are, unfortunately, many who will hear the truth of these words and turn from them, letting their hearts wax cold, believing that only grace and being nice will suffice, because, "God knows my heart."

Jeremiah 17:9 *The heart is deceitful above all things, and desperately sick; who can understand it?*

Hebrews 10:26 *For if we go on sinning deliberately after receiving the knowledge of the truth, there no longer remains a sacrifice for sins,*

2 Peter 2:20-22 *For if, after they have escaped the defilements of the world through the knowledge of our Lord and Savior Jesus Christ, they are again entangled in them and overcome, the last state has become worse for them than the first. For it would have been better for them never to have known the way of righteousness than after knowing it to turn back from the holy commandment delivered to them. What the true proverb says has happened to them: "The dog returns to its own vomit, and the sow, after washing herself, returns to wallow in the* *mire."* Sorry.

Hopefully, though, this book has achieved its goal. You have concluded that the whole Bible still applies and is factual today, and that following the law is God's Love Language. If I have communicated correctly, then you would also realize that the Bible needs to be used with a Hebrew mindset. To be properly understood, verses need to be used and applied in context.

So, what is the second half of this warning? When you find out that we as believers have been deceived for generations, you start to question everything else and rightly so! Vaccines, food companies, 9/11, and Flat Earth are very important, informative, interesting and eye-opening when you look into them. My warning is, do not get so involved with debunking reality that you lose focus on the scriptures. Also, use discernment when you are investigating. There are many out there that would have you question the divinity of Yeshua as the Savior!

Conspiracies like the serpent seed theory, RH-blood types, and a female holy spirit are dangerous and not scriptural. They feed the flesh and not the soul. I would also recommend avoiding the topic of the race of Yeshua and the missing tribes. We have already covered in the chapter, *We Are Gentiles...Right?* that it doesn't matter what you were born into but who you were reborn into. There is a particular sect of people who think that because of their skin color they are chosen and special. This couldn't be further from the scriptures and gives an excuse to breed hate and division.

Please don't get caught up in the pronunciation of Yeshua or YHWH. Most of us in the Torah community call it "sacred naming," and to be honest, it's annoying. It is off-putting to everyone and comes across rude and elitist sometimes. There are plenty of videos on YouTube that go over why this is a completely silly practice. Two of the best ones I have seen are called, "Lies About the Name Jesus" and "How Yeshua Became Jesus" by *Unlearn the Lies*. It is very difficult to determine what a proper pronunciation of YHWH/YHVH is with only four letters. However, I can tell you this, do not believe the internet saying that Jesus came from Zeus, and it doesn't mean earth pig. Don't believe every meme you read!

It's also been noted by many that once you leave "Christianity" some tend to go right over to complete Judaism. Do not do that either. Judah only has one half of the equation and has added to their doctrine with the Talmud as well. The Talmud, are the laws and rules that Jesus and the Apostles spoke out about in the first place. It is not the Torah. This is why it is a narrow path. It is faith and grace through Yeshua that saves you. The obedience of following the Torah are the works of the spirit. Christianity is all faith and grace, and Judaism is all works. Welcome to the narrow road between.

There is also a belief that there are only seven laws that non-Jews need to follow, the Noahide Laws. These laws on the surface sound as if they are from scripture. There is no biblical proof that YHWH gave separate laws to Noah after the flood for non-Jews. At that time, there were no Jews or non-Jews. There was only the one nation of Israel, a line carried on by Noah and his family.

When you first come to the truth of Torah Observance, you want to share it with the whole world. You may become what we have come to call a "Torah Terrorist." I believe everyone goes through this. You try to inform your family and friends by bringing the truth into the light. You may become aggressive and self-righteous. You may even start to hate Christianity. You may try to correct or attack any posts on social media you see about bacon, Christmas, Easter, or grace-only theology. I did it, and from experience, let me tell you, the only thing it did was alienate my family and friends even more.

People who do not see the truth and may not ever will start to make accusations. I have been accused of being in a cult. I have been asked if I was becoming Jewish or Muslim. I have been accused of being brainwashed and once being a Satanist. Yeah, that one confused me too. How one can be a Satanist by trying to obey the laws of YHWH still has me scratching my head. People who don't agree with our beliefs say we are practicing witchcraft. Again, this confuses me. There are those who will accuse you of going back into bondage. We covered that it isn't scriptural either. You may be accused of being carnal hearted or trying to belittle Yeshua's sacrifice. It can make you angry and make you feel lonely.

Luke 12:53 The father shall be divided against the son, and the son against the father; the mother against the daughter, and the daughter against the mother; the mother in law against her daughter in law, and the daughter in law against her mother in law.

Matthew 10:35 For I am come to set a man at variance against his father, and the daughter against her mother, and the daughter in law against her mother in law.

Unfortunately, Yeshua said this would happen. I believe it is meant to strengthen you for the great falling away of the church, so that you will know who may turn against you when the NWO goes after the remnant, as foretold in Matthew and Revelations.

Matthew 24:9 Then shall they deliver you up to be afflicted, and shall kill you: and ye shall be hated of all nations for my name's sake. And then shall many be offended, and shall betray one another, and shall hate one another. And many false prophets shall rise, and shall deceive And because iniquity shall abound, the love of many shall wax cold. But he that shall endure unto the end, the same shall be saved.

Take heart—you are not alone in spirit. Many of us now walk the narrow path alone or with only our spouses or children. A great tool to find like-minded people is the fellowship finder. You can look on *NYSTV.org* or *119ministries* to find a map of like-minded people looking for fellowship.

Do not give into your doubt, fear, or your flesh. As my husband says, do not be faithful to your fear. Remember, "Do not fear," is stated three hundred and sixty-five times in the Bible, one for every day of the year! Following the Torah means obedience to YHWH and not yourself. It means to crucify your flesh daily.

Shalom.

GREAT RESOURCES FOR HELP IN UNDERSTANDING TORAH:

<u>YouTube channels and web pages</u>

- 119ministries: testeverything.net

- New2Torah: new2torah.com

- Unlearn the lies: unlearnthelies.com

- NYSTV: nystv.org

- Torah family: Torahfamily.org

- Triumph in Truth: email: connect@triumphfamily.tv

- My House Ministries: myhouseministries.net

RECIPES

All recipes are written to American measure and temperature standards.

Thank you, Mel and Nikki, for your contributions. For more of Greg's delicious Biblically clean recipes, you can find him on Facebook and Instagram under Torah Chef@cheftorah on Twitter and his YouTube channel, Torah Chef (coming soon!).

Mel's Fried Matzo

Shared by Mel Varner

½ cup of butter
1 ½ cups of hot water
2 t. Salt
2 Tbsp gluten
2 Tbsp honey
Handful of flax
Flour

Directions:

Combine all ingredients, except for flour, in a bowl and stir thoroughly. Add handfuls of flour gradually. Beat mixture into a workable dough (pulls away from the bowl). Knead for 5-10 minutes. Divide into even portions and flatten. Fry in hot olive oil and slather with butter.

Nikki's Matzo Toffee

Shared by Nikki Sharp

2 cups coarsely crumbled matzo crackers
1 ½ cups sliced almonds
½ cup (1 stick) of unsalted butter
½ cup packed light brown sugar
½ t of salt
2 cups semi-sweet chocolate chips

Directions:

Preheat oven to 325 degrees. Line a large baking sheet with parchment paper. In a bowl, toss matzo and almonds together. In a saucepan, bring butter, sugar, salt, and 2 tablespoons of water to a boil over medium heat, stirring constantly. Working quickly, toss the matzo and butter mixtures together. With a spatula, carefully spread the mixture onto the baking sheet. Bake in the oven for 30 minutes. Remove from oven and while still hot, place chocolate chips on to melt. Refrigerate until chocolate has set, break into pieces, and enjoy!

Nikki's Smoked Passover Lamb

Shared by Nikki Sharp

3-4 handsful of hickory chips
1 3-4 Rack of Lamb
3 sprigs of rosemary, roughly chopped
4 Tbsp kosher or coarse salt
4 Tbsp Fresh Ground Pepper
Acidic liquid (pineapple juice, apple juice, apple cider vinegar, Coca-Cola®, etc.)
Suggested: Mrs. Dash® with garlic and herb or extra spicy with red pepper.

Directions:

Soak the lamb overnight in the acidic liquid of your choice.

Soak hickory chips in hot water for 45-60 minutes minimum. Put Chips in a smoker and heat to 225 degrees. Rub rack of lamb with salt, pepper, and rosemary (optional Mrs. Dash). Place in smoker, close lid. Smoke for 1 ½ -2 hours or longer as needed. Internal temperature for a medium-rare rack is 155 F. Smoke longer for more doneness. Remove from grill, cover with tin foil, and let rest for 10 minutes.

TIP: to keep meat from drying get the juice of your choice and baste a few times while smoking.

Easy Challah Bread

Shared by Greg Cornelius "Torah Chef"

1 1/2 cups to 2 cups warm water
3 tablespoons dry activated yeast
1/2 cup plus 1 tablespoon sugar
6 cups plus 1 cup all-purpose flour
1 tablespoon salt
3 large eggs plus 1 yolk, beaten (save the white for topping)
1/2 cup melted butter (You may Substitute coconut oil or olive oil)
sesame seeds for topping

Directions:

In a small bowl, dissolve yeast with 1 tablespoon sugar in warm water; set aside.

In a separate large bowl, whisk together 6 cups flour, 1/2 cup sugar and salt.

Add beaten eggs and the water with dissolved yeast and sugar to the large bowl of flour.

Stir in melted butter and mix well with a wooden spoon. Add to a stand mixer with dough hook, or a lightly floured surface for kneading. You may use the reserved flour as needed, but the dough should remain somewhat sticky. Knead for 10 minutes

Oil a large bowl, then place dough into bowl flipping it over to make sure it is covered with the oil. Cover with a towel and let the dough rise until doubled in bulk.

Punch down, knead one or two times and then divide dough in half.

Divide each half into 3 equal strands (or more depending on how intricate you want it) and braid, pinching each end to seal

Place each braided loaf on a parchment or silicone mat lined cookie sheet, and cover with a dry towel and let rise a second time until loaves are double in size.

Preheat oven to 350 degrees. Brush each loaf with egg white, and sprinkle sesame seeds if you wish.

Bake for about 30 minutes or until bread is golden brown on the surface. Let cool completely before slicing

Roast leg of Lamb au Jus

Shared by Greg Cornelius "Torah Chef"

3-4-pound lamb leg BRT (boned, rolled and tied)
4 Cloves of garlic, crushed
3 TB kosher salt
1 TB coarse ground black pepper
2 sprigs fresh rosemary (woody stems removed)
2 sprigs fresh thyme (woody stems removed)
2 Tsp fresh or dried oregano
1 lemon, zest and juice
2 TB olive oil
2 ribs celery- 1" rough chop
1 large carrot - 1" rough chop
1 medium onion roughly chop
1 cup chicken or beef stock

Directions:

Preheat oven to 325 degrees.

In a food processor combine herbs, garlic, salt, pepper, zest, lemon juice, and olive oil. This should form a loose paste. Rub generously onto the lamb leg. In a roasting pan, place the carrot, celery, and onions in the bottom of the pan, and the lamb leg on top. Roast at 325° 45 minutes and test for doneness. I cook to an internal temperature of 140°, which will be medium by the time the roast rests. When the roast is to the desired doneness, set aside to rest for 30 minutes. While the roast is resting, add stock to the roasting pan and vegetables. Simmer for 15 minutes while scraping the browned bits from the pan. Add salt and pepper to taste. Strain and serve with thinly sliced lamb.

Braised Brisket

Shared by Greg Cornelius "Torah Chef"

3-4# brisket 1st cut/flat
1 cup dry red wine
1 yellow onion, sliced
2 medium shallots, sliced thin
2 cloves garlic, crushed
1 sprig thyme, or 1 tsp dry thyme
1 bay leaf
2 large carrots, cut in 3/4" pieces
2 ribs celery cut in 1" sections
1 TB sea salt or kosher salt
1 TB black pepper
2 tsp hungarian paprika
1 TB dijon mustard
2 TB olive oil
1.5 c water
1 TB cornstarch

Directions:

Preheat oven to 350 degrees

Season brisket with salt, pepper, paprika. Place seasoned brisket in a roasting pan with 1 TB oil, uncovered in a 350° oven. Roast for 15 minutes, then turn and roast another 15 minutes. Add vegetables, thyme, bay leaf, red wine, mustard, and 1 cup water. Cover and cook for 30 more minutes. Stir the vegetables and open the cover 1/2" so some of the liquid can evaporate and roast for 2 more hours, or until brisket is tender. Remove brisket from the vegetables and braising liquid to allow to cool for slicing. Bring the vegetables and sauce to a simmer, add salt and pepper to taste. Stir in 1/2c water and cornstarch mixture to thicken. Serve with sliced brisket.

Ropa Vieja

Shared by Greg Cornelius "Torah Chef"

"Old Clothes" This classic Cuban dish pairs traditionally with rice, black beans and sweet plantains.

2.5 # flank steak (you can substitute skirt or Chuck)
1 15 oz can crushed tomatoes
1 rib celery diced
1 carrot, diced
1 TB tomato paste
1 lime, juiced
4 cloves garlic, minced
2 tsp ground cumin
2 tsp oregano leaf (preferably Mexican)
1 tsp smoked paprika
1 tsp spanish paprika
Sea salt to taste
2 bell peppers (1 red, 1 green), sliced 1/2 inch thick
1 Large onion, thinly sliced
1 small jar Manzanilla olives with pimento, halved
2 tsp ground black pepper
1 TB olive oil
Cooked white rice for serving

Directions:

Heat a heavy bottomed deep saucepan over medium high heat, add olive oil. Salt and pepper the beef, and sear 2-3 minutes on each side. Remove the browned meat and set aside. Add garlic, carrots, onion, celery, and cook until slightly soft. Add tomato paste, tomatoes, beef, olives, spices, and lime juice. Reduce to low heat and cover. Cook for 3 hours or until meat shreds easily. Serve with rice

Easier version. Throw it all in the crock pot and cook low for 8 hours. Shred and serve (great for Sabbath Day).

Hummus

Shared by Greg Cornelius "Torah Chef"

1 15 oz can chickpeas (or 1.5c cooked chickpeas)
1/2 tsp baking soda
Juice of 1 lemon (fresh is best)
1/2 c tahini
2 cloves garlic, smashed
2 Tb good extra virgin olive oil
1/2 tsp cumin
2 Tb cold water
1 tsp salt

Directions:

Drain and rinse the chickpeas. Boil in just enough water to cover with 1/2 tsp baking soda. This is the trick to soft chickpeas to make a very smooth hummus. Simmer for 20 minutes. Drain and rinse with cold water.

In a food processor combine chickpeas, garlic, lemon juice, salt, cumin, tahini. Puree until well combined. Add cold water and drizzle in olive oil while running. It should be a smooth paste.

Garnish with fresh parsley, Za'atar®, crushed pepper, olive oil or any other toppings of choice. I like to serve with warm pita.

Unleavened Bread (Sweet version)

Shared by Stephanie Cornelius

1 cup almond flour
1 cup organic all-purpose flour (for gluten free
substitute 1:1 Gluten free baking flour)
1/4 cup honey
3/4 cup melted butter (coconut oil may be
substituted)
1/4 cup water
1 tbsp fresh dried ground rosemary

Directions:

Preheat oven to 350 degrees

Combine all ingredients, kneading until smooth.
Roll out with a rolling pin on a lightly floured
surface and cut into strips (or whatever shape you
desire). Place on parchment or silicone mat lined
baking sheet and bake @350 for 17 min. Let cool
completely before serving.

ACKNOWLEDGEMENTS

First and foremost, I want to thank YHWH for giving His perfect laws to us. I want to thank Yeshua for taking my sins as His own and saving me from them. I want to thank them both for loving me. Thank you, YHWH, for your perfect instruction on how love you.

I want to thank my husband and children for supporting me. Thank you, James, for always being there for me, supporting me and loving me, no matter what.

I want to thank my extended family Mel, Kevin, Richard, Kc, Kevin, Nikki, Doc, and Mark for supporting me and allowing me to bounce ideas and research off of them. Without you all, I would not have been able to do this. You are my mishpachah and brothers and sisters in Yeshua.

I would like to say a special thanks to Dana Ellis for helping me to edit my book. As a skilled published author yourself, your help and feedback were invaluable. I would like to also say a thank you to Christine Sterling Bortner for her advice as a published author of multiple books, her formatting skills, and recommending Virginia McKevitt for my beautiful cover design. Virginia, thank you so much for making my vision come to life and taking time from your writing to do so.

I would like to say a special thank you to my proofreader, Laura Clark. I wish I had found you sooner, but your assistance with the second edition has helped me so much in growing as a writer and making my book the best possible for the readers.

I want to thank *NYSTV*, Jon Pounders, David and Donna Carrico, Jake Grant, John and Patricia Hall for giving me a place to fellowship and learn every week.

Thank you, Zach Baur, for your wonderful and informative videos on *New2Torah*.

I would also like to say a special thanks to Rob Skiba. I watched your video on Nimrod from your conference in Amsterdam. Had you not mentioned the truth of Torah, I would not have been compelled to search out the truth for myself. So, again, thank you and keep fighting the good fight.

Thank you, the reader, for taking the time to read my book and see it through to the end. I hope and pray this opens the doors to a better understanding of the Bible and the love language of YHWH.

I want to state in this book, I am not a college educated theologian. I am a wife, a mother, and I have probably sinned more than most. However, thankfully, I have the love and forgiveness of Yeshua. I was saved and baptized at fourteen years old in a Freewill Baptist Church. Like most people who grew up in church, I was taught there is nothing needed to receive this forgiveness but to pray the sinner's prayer, receive Jesus and go back to normal life with a Teflon sin barrier that protects you from the evil of sin and nothing will ever stick again. Although no one ever taught me what sin was, I knew it no longer applied to me.

Like any person with a free pass, I took full and total advantage. I committed almost every sin and then some over and over again, thinking that because I was saved, I was safe. I didn't even need to read the Bible or worship God because, hey I was saved. I would crack open my mostly ignored Bible, pray or go to church only when I needed something from Him. I did this for the better part of twenty years. I had reduced the creator's existence, the savior of this world and my soul, to a good luck charm. I reduced the Bible, His word and direction to a magic eight ball! If I got what I wanted, then I would thank him, and most times I did not. I started to question His very existence. *If Jesus loved me enough to die for my sins then why doesn't He love me enough to provide me with better clothes, a healthier body, or give me a great idea that I can use to get rich and take care of my kids?*

I watched prosperity preachers telling me how to live my best life now, and if I only gave a thousand dollars I didn't have, I would plant a seed that would blossom and make me rich. I would give money or donations to people with the sole purpose of hoping that God would see what I did and give me a blessing that I could retire on. It was the most selfish and one-sided "relationship" with my savior and creator. And millions of people are still in this same type of relationship with Him.

My goal for this book is to use the Bible to determine what God's love language is and how we can speak it. I am not a teacher. I don't have all the answers. I am sharing the ones I have found. I am always searching for deeper understanding and truth. I want to make it very clear. I am not a teacher. I am a student. I also want to state unequivocally, THERE IS NO WAY TO EARN SALVATION. How we behave and act after we receive the gift of salvation are the fruits of it. How we behave and act after salvation is our testimony to the world. Salvation is the root and obedience is the fruit.

Hosea 4:6 *My people are destroyed for lack of knowledge; because you have rejected knowledge, I reject you from being a priest to me. And since you have forgotten the law of your God, I also will forget your children.*

Made in the USA
Coppell, TX
16 January 2020